Alexander
Höss-Knakal

Fairytale Cooking

DELICIOUS DISHES INSPIRED BY
THE LITTLE MERMAID, CINDERELLA, ALADDIN,
AND OTHER CLASSIC CHARACTERS

Photography by Melina Kutelas

Skyhorse Publishing

Contents

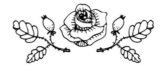

Cinderella
141

The Snow Queen
171

Spellbinding
Fairytale Menus

Preface

Fairytales. You might be drawn into their magic by lovingly designed tomes, carefully printed on old paper that rustles promisingly as you turn the pages. Their words easily whisk us away into strange, enchanted, yet familiar worlds contained between something as simple as two book covers.

These timeless stories, some of which date back hundreds of years, continue to be popular across generations, from the very young to the old. Perhaps this is because they evoke a sense of longing in us for the bliss of being snuggled up on a parent's or grandparent's lap, just listening. Or perhaps we seek the reassurance that familiar words, heard over and over again, can offer. Or perhaps it is because the values fairytales teach us – the importance of family and friendship, patience, persistence, courage, and tolerance – are just as timeless as the stories themselves. Even more, they are as relevant and much needed in our modern societies as they have ever been. The heroes and heroines we meet in fairytales give us courage – just think of Gerda, in *The Snow Queen*, who travels the world searching for her best friend, Kai. Or the Little Mermaid, who does not hesitate to take enormous risks, seeking to fulfill her dream without knowing whether she will succeed.

This timeless nature is precisely what fairytales and cooking have in common – the wisdom of fairytales and the soul of good cooking can last for centuries. Stories and recipes are passed on from one generation to the next; from parents to children and from children to grandchildren. Just like treasured stories, favorite dishes and recipes never go out of fashion either: as soon as the familiar aroma of a traditional Sunday roast wafts through the home, it evokes an irresistible feeling of delight.

But fairytales and recipes are also both capable of transporting us into foreign worlds. Where else but in the kitchen can we travel to different countries and cultures in the course of just a single meal? We invite you to enjoy an exotic candlelight feast straight out of the Arabian Nights. Let Little Red Riding Hood take you on a culinary stroll through the wood, or allow yourself to be whisked away to an enchanted castle by a menu of fine dining.

Take an even closer look and you'll discover another similarity. Both cooking and stories can marry contrasting elements to create surprisingly harmonious pairings. Or would anybody doubt that pancakes with bacon and maple syrup are the ultimate flavor explosion? Just ask Beauty and the Beast . . . they'd certainly agree that opposites can be a marriage made in heaven.

Finally, fairytales and cooking have yet another thing in common. When we become engrossed in a good story, our mind gets carried away by the words and we forget about time. The same thing can happen when we cook. If you're attentive to it, you'll soon notice that chopping vegetables, kneading dough, and stirring steaming pots all have a very soothing, entrancing quality. We're able to experience aromas, flavors, and textures with all of our senses, and we can share them with our guests to tell them the most delightful culinary stories.

If this inspires you to rediscover your favorite childhood fairytales, we invite you to start by making yourself comfortable on your sofa with this book. Then transport the recipes into your kitchen to create your own culinary wonderland.

We hope you'll enjoy this book.

Julia Bauer, Alexander Höss-Knakal, and Melina Kutelas

Little Red Riding Hood and The Wolf

nce upon a time, there was a sweet little girl who was adored by everyone who looked at her. But most of all she was dearest to the heart of her grandmother, and there was nothing the grandmother wouldn't have given to the child. Once she gave the girl a red velvet cape, and because it suited her so well and she never wanted to take it off, she was always called Little Red Riding Hood. One day the girl's mother said to her, 'Come, Little Red Riding Hood, here is a piece of cake and a bottle of wine, take them to your grandmother. She is ill and weak and will be happy to have them. Set out before it gets hot, and once you are on your way be careful and do not run off the path, or you might fall and break the bottle, and then your grandmother will not have anything. And when you go into her home do not forget to say good morning and do not peep into every corner before you say it.'

'I will do everything right,' promised Little Red Riding Hood. The grandmother lived out in the wood, half an hour's walk from the village. When Little Red Riding Hood entered the wood, she ran across the Wolf. Little Red Riding Hood did not know how wicked a creature he was and therefore was not afraid of him. 'Good morning, Little Red Riding Hood,' said the Wolf. 'Thank you, Wolf,' answered the girl. 'Where are you off to so early in the day, Little Red Riding Hood?' 'To see my grandmother.' 'And what have you got in your apron?' 'Wine and cake we baked yesterday so that my poor, weak grandmother would have

something nice. Good food will help her get well again.' 'And where does your grandmother live, Little Red Riding Hood?' 'Just another quarter of an hour's walk further into the wood. Her house stands under the three large oak trees. Down there near the nut hedges. You surely must know it,' said Little Red Riding Hood. The Wolf thought to himself, *What a tender young thing, she'll make a nice mouthful. She'll taste even better than the old woman. But I'll have to be crafty about this to catch them both.* So he walked with Little Red Riding Hood for a short while and then said, 'Little Red Riding Hood, look at the pretty flowers growing all around us. Why don't you have a look? And I believe you do not even hear how sweetly the little birds are singing! You just walk along as if you were going to school, yet it is so beautiful here in the wood.'

Little Red Riding Hood raised her eyes, and when she saw the rays of sunlight dancing between the trees and the pretty flowers growing everywhere, she said, 'I suppose Grandmother will be happy if I bring her a bunch of fresh flowers. It's early in the day so I will still get there in time.' And so she ran off the path to look for flowers. As soon as she had picked one, she was certain there would be an even lovelier one a little further on, and this is how she got ever more deeply into the wood. But the Wolf went straight to the grandmother's house and knocked on the door. 'Who is there?' 'Little Red Riding Hood, Grandmother, I have cake and wine for you. Open the door,' said the Wolf, disguising his voice. 'Just press the latch, the door is open,' said Grandmother, 'I'm too weak and cannot get up.' The Wolf pressed down the latch,

> 'Grandmother, I have cake and wine for you. Open the door,' said the Wolf, disguising his voice.

the door sprang open, and he went straight to Grandmother's bed, not saying a word, and devoured her entirely. Then he put on her clothes and her cap. He laid down in her bed and drew the curtains.

Meanwhile, Little Red Riding Hood was still picking flowers, and when she had gathered so many that she could not carry any more, she remembered her grandmother and set out again on her way to her house. She was surprised to find the door standing open, and when she entered the house, it felt very strange. She said to herself, 'Oh dear, I feel so anxious here today, when usually I like being with Grandmother so much.' She called out, 'Good morning,' but received no answer. So she went to the bed and drew back the curtains. There was Grandmother with her cap pulled down over her face, and she looked very strange. 'Oh, Grandmother,' she said, 'what big ears you have!' 'The better to hear you with.' 'Oh, Grandmother, what big eyes you have!' 'The better to see you with.' 'Oh, Grandmother, what big hands you have!' 'The better to grab you with.' 'But, Grandmother, what a terribly big mouth you have!' 'The better to eat you with!' No sooner had the Wolf said this than he bounded out of the bed and devoured Little Red Riding Hood as well.

Satiated, the Wolf went to lie down in the bed again. He fell asleep and began to snore loudly. It happened that a huntsman passed the house and thought to himself, *How the old woman is snoring! I'd better see whether she is in need of anything.*

He entered the house, and when he came to the bed, he saw that the Wolf was lying in it. 'So this is where I find you, you old sinner,' he said. 'I've been looking for you for a long time.' He raised his rifle and was going to shoot the Wolf, but then it struck him that the Wolf might have eaten the grandmother and that she could still be saved. So he did not fire, but instead took a pair of scissors and began to cut the sleeping Wolf's belly open. After just a few snips he saw a red hood shining, and after a few more the little girl jumped out and cried, 'Oh, how frightened I have been. It was so dark inside the Wolf!' Grandmother also came out alive, but scarcely able to breathe. Little Red Riding Hood quickly fetched some large stones with which they filled the Wolf's belly. When the

Wolf finally awoke, he wanted to run away, but the stones were so heavy that he collapsed at once and died.

How relieved and delighted all three were! The huntsman drew off the Wolf's skin and took it home. Grandmother ate the cake and drank the wine Little Red Riding Hood had brought her, and she soon recovered. But Little Red Riding Hood thought to herself, *For as long as I live, I'll never again stray off the path and into the wood when my mother has forbidden it.*

It is also said that once, when Little Red Riding Hood was again taking a cake to her old grandmother, another Wolf tried to entice her away from her path. But Little Red Riding Hood was on her guard and would not stray. She told Grandmother that she had met a Wolf again, who had said good morning to her, but with such a wicked look in his eyes that she was sure he would have eaten her there and then had they not been on a public road. 'Come inside,' said Grandmother. 'Let's lock the door so that he cannot get in.' Soon after, the Wolf knocked on the door and, disguising his voice, called, 'Open the door, Grandmother, it's me, Little Red Riding Hood, bringing you cake.' But Little Red Riding Hood and Grandmother did not answer, nor did they open the door. So the old greybeard circled the house a few times and finally jumped on the roof, intending to wait until Little Red Riding Hood would go home in the evening. Then he thought he could track her and devour her in the darkness. But Grandmother realized what the Wolf was planning. Outside the house was a large stone trough, and she told the girl, 'I made sausages yesterday. Little Red Riding Hood, take this bucket and pour the water in which I boiled them into the trough.' Little Red Riding Hood worked until the entire large trough was full. The enticing smell of the sausages reached the Wolf, and he sniffed and looked down. Greedily, he stretched out his neck so far that he could no longer hold his footing. He started to slide off the roof straight down into the big trough, where he drowned. Little Red Riding Hood walked home happily, and no one ever did her any harm again in her life.

An enchanting walk in the forest

Stepping across fragrant green mosses, taking in the earthy scent of mushrooms and the damp coolness of ancient trees – a walk in the forest is a veritable feast for all our senses. Not only that, but it also inspires endless creativity in the kitchen. We can't wait to taste some of the delicacies Little Red Riding Hood has collected in her basket!

APPETIZER

Button mushroom flatbread with hazelnut pesto

MAIN COURSE

Saddle of venison with carrot purée and porcini mushrooms

DESSERT

Mini red wine cupcakes with a cheesecake heart

Button mushroom flatbread with hazelnut pesto

Serves 4

INGREDIENTS

For the dough:
250 g (9 oz/1⅔ cups) plain
  (all-purpose) flour
10 g (¼ oz) fresh yeast
150 ml (5 fl oz) lukewarm water
2 tbsp olive oil
1 tsp salt

For the topping:
200 g (7 oz) button mushrooms
1 lemon
2 tbsp olive oil
Salt
Freshly ground black pepper
1 tsp coriander seeds
175 g (6 oz/¾ cup) cream cheese

For the hazelnut pesto:
2 garlic cloves
50 g (1¾ oz/⅓ cup) hazelnuts
30 g (1 oz) pecorino cheese
15 g (½ oz/¼ cup) basil leaves
15 g (½ oz/¾ cup) parsley leaves
125 ml (4 fl oz/½ cup) olive oil

Also:
Flour for dusting

To make the dough, sift the flour onto your clean countertop and make a well in the center. Dissolve the yeast in the lukewarm water. Pour the yeasted water into the well. Add the olive oil and salt and knead to make a smooth dough. Transfer the dough to a mixing bowl, cover with plastic wrap, and leave to rise for about 1 hour.

Preheat the oven to 240°C (475°F). Line a baking tray with baking paper. Punch down the dough, dust your counter with flour, and roll the dough out into an oval 30 x 20 cm (12 x 8 inches) in size and 2–3 mm (1/16–1/8 inches) thick.

For the topping, trim and slice the mushrooms. Halve and juice the lemon. Combine the sliced mushrooms with the lemon juice, olive oil, salt, and pepper and set aside to marinate for 10 minutes. Finely crush the coriander seeds in a mortar and pestle and toss in with the mushrooms. Stir salt and pepper into the cream cheese and spread the mixture on the rolled-out dough, leaving a margin of about 1 cm (½ inch). Spread the mushrooms evenly on top. Bake in the preheated oven (middle rack) until golden brown, about 15–20 minutes.

Meanwhile, peel and crush the garlic for the hazelnut pesto. Coarsely chop the hazelnuts and dry-roast them lightly in a frying pan. Set aside to cool. Coarsely grate the pecorino cheese. Rinse and shake the herbs dry, then combine them with the grated cheese and olive oil and blend until smooth. Finally, fold in the hazelnuts and garlic. Cut the flatbread into slices and serve together with the hazelnut pesto.

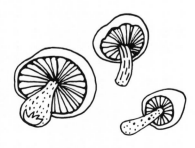

Ricotta gnocchi with sage

Serves 4

INGREDIENTS

80 g (2¾ oz) full-flavored
   hard cheese
500 g (1 lb 2 oz) ricotta cheese
Salt
Freshly ground black pepper
300 g (10½ oz/2 cups) plain
   (all-purpose) flour
4 eggs
4 sage sprigs
100 g (3½ oz) butter

Also:
Flour for dusting
1 orange
30 g (1 oz) full-flavored
   hard cheese

For the dough, finely grate the hard cheese. Combine the ricotta, salt, pepper, flour, eggs, and grated cheese in a bowl and mix well. Cover the bowl and refrigerate the gnocchi mixture for 1 hour.

Next, divide the dough into three equal portions on a lightly floured surface. Roll each of the portions into logs about 1 cm (½ inch) thick. Use a sharp knife to cut the logs into 1 cm (½ inch) pieces. Bring plenty of salted water to the boil in a large pot. Add the gnocchi, reduce the heat to low, and simmer for about 3 minutes.

Meanwhile, rinse the sage and shake dry. Heat the butter and sage in a large frying pan until the butter starts to brown.

Use a slotted spoon to remove the gnocchi from the saucepan. Drain well and toss with the browned sage butter. Wash the orange under hot water and pat dry. Finely peel the zest and cut into very fine matchsticks. Grate the hard cheese. Divide the gnocchi and sage butter among plates. Garnish with the orange zest and grated cheese and serve with a sprinkle of freshly grated black pepper.

Chanterelle frittata

Serves 4

INGREDIENTS

*200 g (7 oz) chanterelle
  or shiitake mushrooms
2 French shallots
1 bunch chives
4 cherry tomatoes
1 lemon
50 ml (1½ fl oz) heavy cream
4 eggs
250 g (9 oz) cottage cheese
Salt
Freshly ground black pepper
2 tbsp olive oil, divided*

Also:
*Sea salt for sprinkling
Bread for serving*

Clean the mushrooms with a knife and a damp cloth. Halve the larger mushrooms. Peel and finely dice the shallots. Rinse the chives, shake off any excess water, and slice thinly. Wash and slice the cherry tomatoes. Wash the lemon under hot water and pat dry. Finely peel the zest and cut into very fine matchsticks.

Preheat the oven to 200°C (400°F). Whisk the cream, eggs, and cottage cheese until well combined and season with salt and pepper. Heat 1 tbsp olive oil in a flameproof frying pan (about 26 cm/10½ inches in diameter). Add the egg mixture and fry for about 1 minute. Top with the sliced tomatoes, then transfer the pan to the preheated oven (bottom rack) and cook the frittata until done, about 20 minutes.

Meanwhile, heat the remaining olive oil in another pan. Add the mushrooms and shallots and sear for a few minutes. Season with salt and pepper. Add the chives and lemon zest, toss to combine, and keep warm.

Top the cooked frittata with the mushrooms. Sprinkle with sea salt and serve with bread.

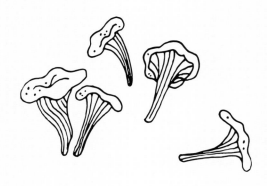

19

The world's best bread

Makes 1 loaf (24 cm/9½ inches)

INGREDIENTS

For the sourdough:
30 ml (1 fl oz) lukewarm water
7 g (¼ oz) sourdough starter
40 g (1½ oz) rye flour

For the pre-ferment:
½ tsp dry yeast
70 ml (2¼ fl oz) lukewarm water
60 g (2¼ oz) spelt flour

For the bread dough:
270 ml (9½ fl oz) lukewarm water
100 g (3½ oz/⅔ cup) whole
  wheat flour
50 g (1¾ oz) rye flour
190 g (6¾ oz) spelt flour
15 g (½ oz) salt

Also:
Flour for dusting

The day before baking, combine the water, sourdough starter, and rye flour to make the sourdough. Cover with plastic wrap and set aside at room temperature for 24 hours to allow the dough to develop.

For the pre-ferment, combine the dry yeast, water, and spelt flour in a bowl. Cover and leave to rest in the refrigerator for 12 hours.

The next day, mix the sourdough and the pre-ferment with the lukewarm water in a bowl to make the bread dough. Add the whole wheat flour, rye flour, spelt flour, and salt and knead everything slowly to make a homogeneous mixture. Cover the dough and leave to rise at room temperature for about 3 hours. If you leave it for longer and it rises too much, punch the dough down repeatedly. Knead the dough again once it has risen.

Line a lidded casserole dish (about 24 cm/9½ inches in diameter) with baking paper. Transfer the dough to the dish. Dust with a little flour, press flat, and put the lid on. Leave to proof at room temperature for about 1 hour.

Meanwhile, preheat the oven to 250°C (500°F). Transfer the dish to the preheated oven with the lid on (bottom rack) and bake the bread for 20 minutes. Remove the lid and lift the bread out of the dish together with the baking paper. Place the bread on a baking tray and continue to bake until done, about another 20 minutes. Remove the bread from the oven and set it aside to cool on a wire rack.

Saddle of venison with carrot purée and porcini mushrooms

Serves 4

INGREDIENTS

For the carrot purée:
1 piece fresh ginger
  (about 1 cm/½ inch)
300 g (10½ oz) carrots
1 orange
150 ml (5 fl oz) heavy cream
Salt
Freshly grated nutmeg

For the saddle of venison:
600 g (1 lb 5 oz) kitchen-ready
  saddle of venison (deboned)
Salt
1 tsp juniper berries
1 tsp black peppercorns
2 tbsp olive oil
150 ml (5 fl oz) red wine
500 ml (17 fl oz/2 cups) venison
  (or veal) stock
2 tbsp cranberries (from a jar)

For the mushrooms:
2 parsley sprigs
200 g (7 oz) fresh porcini
  mushrooms
1 tbsp olive oil
Salt

Also:
Sea salt for sprinkling
Organic, unsprayed nasturtium
  leaves for garnish

For the carrot purée, peel and mince the ginger. Peel and finely dice the carrot. Halve and juice the orange. Add the ginger, carrots, orange juice, and cream to a small saucepan and season with salt and nutmeg. Bring everything to a boil, cover, and simmer until soft over a low heat, about 15 minutes. Blend until smooth with a hand-held blender.

For the saddle of venison, preheat the oven to 120°C (235°F). Season the meat with salt. Finely crush the juniper berries and peppercorns in a mortar and pestle and rub the saddle of venison all over with the crushed spices.

For the mushrooms, rinse the parsley, shake off any excess water, and thinly slice the leaves. Clean and trim the mushrooms and cut them into 5 mm (¼ inch) slices. Heat the olive oil in a frying pan. Add the mushrooms and fry until golden. Season with salt and toss with the parsley.

Meanwhile, heat the olive oil for the venison in a large frying pan. Add the meat and sear all over. Transfer the venison to a baking tray and place inside the preheated oven (middle rack). Cook until medium rare, about 5 minutes. Meanwhile, deglaze the pan with the red wine and simmer to reduce. Stir in the venison stock and cranberries. Bring everything to a boil and simmer again to reduce a little.

Cut the saddle of venison into slices and sprinkle with a little sea salt. Divide the carrot purée, mushrooms, and sliced venison among plates. Drizzle with the gravy and serve garnished with nasturtium leaves.

Nut roast with vegetarian gravy

Makes 1 loaf (about 25 cm/ 10 inches long)

Serves 4–6

INGREDIENTS

For the nut roast:

300 g (10½ oz) mixed nuts
  (e.g. walnuts, hazelnuts,
  cashews, or almonds)
2 carrots (about 200 g/7 oz)
1 onion
2 garlic cloves
2 tbsp olive oil
1 bunch parsley
1 rosemary sprig
2 slices white bread
100 g (3½ oz) grated
  emmental cheese
3 eggs
1 tbsp dijon mustard
½ tsp salt

For the gravy:

1 packet soup vegetables
  (e.g. carrots, celeriac, parsley root/
  Hamburg parsley, leek, and parsley)
100 g (3½ oz) button mushrooms
1 tbsp olive oil
1 tbsp tomato paste
100 ml (3½ fl oz) red wine

Also:

Cornflour (cornstarch)
  for thickening (as needed)

For the nut roast, toast the nuts in a frying pan. Set aside to cool, then chop finely. Peel and coarsely grate the carrot. Peel and finely dice the onion; peel and mince the garlic. Heat the olive oil in a frying pan. Add the onion and garlic and sweat for a few minutes.

Preheat the oven to 180°C (350°F). Rinse the parsley and rosemary and shake dry. Pick off the leaves and chop finely. Cut the bread into very fine cubes. Combine all of the prepared ingredients with the emmental cheese, eggs, mustard, and salt in a bowl.

Line a loaf tin with baking paper. Pour the nut roast mix into the tin and level the top. Bake the nut roast in the preheated oven (bottom rack) for 40–50 minutes – use a toothpick to test for doneness. Remove from the oven and invert onto a serving board.

Meanwhile, make the vegetarian gravy. Wash, trim, and peel (if necessary) the soup vegetables and cut them into small pieces. Clean and thinly slice the mushrooms. Heat the olive oil in a saucepan. Add the soup vegetables and mushrooms and sauté for a few minutes. Stir in the tomato paste and fry briefly. Deglaze everything with the red wine. Simmer for a few minutes to reduce, then stir in 500 ml (17 fl oz/2 cups) water. Simmer for 15–20 minutes. Pass the gravy, including the mushrooms and vegetables, through a sieve. Thicken with a little cornflour if necessary.

Slice the nut roast. Divide the slices among plates and serve with the gravy.

Farm-style potatoes
with sausage

Serves 4

INGREDIENTS

1 kg (2 lb 4 oz) waxy potatoes
Salt
2 garlic cloves
1 large red onion
300 g (10½ oz) parboiled sausage
   (Brunswick or other pork sausage)
2 tbsp sunflower oil
1 tsp caraway seeds
Freshly ground black pepper

Also:
1 lemon
125 g (4½ oz) crème fraîche
   or sour cream
Salt
1 punnet cress or alfalfa
   sprouts, optional
½ bunch parsley

Boil the unpeeled potatoes in a large saucepan with salted water for 15–20 minutes. Drain and set the potatoes aside for 30 minutes to cool. Peel and thinly slice the potatoes.

Meanwhile, peel and thinly slice the garlic and onion. Halve the sausage lengthways and also slice.

Heat the sunflower oil in a large frying pan. Add the sliced potatoes and fry until browned on both sides, about 5 minutes. Stir in the onion, garlic, caraway, and sausage and continue to fry for another few minutes. Season with salt and pepper.

Meanwhile, wash the lemon under hot water, pat dry, and finely grate the zest. For the dip, combine the crème fraîche, lemon zest, and salt. Cut the cress, rinse, and shake dry. Rinse the parsley, shake dry, and coarsely chop the leaves. Garnish the potatoes and sausage with cress or alfalfa sprouts and parsley and serve together with the dip.

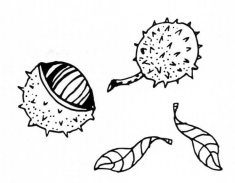

Hearty venison ragout

Serves 4

INGREDIENTS

800 g (1 lb 12 oz) deboned venison
   shoulder (or red deer shoulder)
Salt
Freshly ground black pepper
2 tbsp sunflower oil
2 onions
2 garlic cloves
2 tbsp butter
200 g (7 oz) bacon, diced
1 tbsp tomato paste
2 tbsp cranberries (from a jar)
250 ml (9 fl oz/1 cup)
   full-bodied red wine
500 ml (17 fl oz/2 cups) dark
   venison stock (or beef stock)
4 juniper berries
2 thyme sprigs
1 bay leaf sprig
1 orange
2 carrots
100 g (3½ oz) celeriac
100 g (3½ oz) celery
1 tsp softened butter and 1 tsp flour,
   blended together to make a paste,
   if needed

Rinse the venison shoulder, pat dry, and dice into 3 cm (1¼ inch) cubes. Season the meat with salt and pepper. Heat the sunflower oil in a large saucepan and sear the diced meat over high heat. Remove the meat from the saucepan and set aside. Peel the onion and garlic. Mince the garlic and finely dice the onion.

Melt the butter in the same saucepan. Add the onion, garlic, and bacon and sweat everything. Stir in the tomato paste and fry until it takes on a deeper color. Stir in the cranberries and continue to fry everything for another few minutes. Add the red wine and venison stock and bring everything to a boil over a low heat.

Finely crush the juniper berries in a mortar and pestle. Rinse the thyme, and bay leaves and shake dry. Return the seared meat to the saucepan together with the crushed juniper berries, thyme, and bay leaves. Wash the orange under hot water and pat dry. Grate the zest and add to the stew. Cover the saucepan and continue to cook over a low heat until the meat is tender, about 60–70 minutes.

Meanwhile, peel and dice the carrots and celeriac. Wash and trim the celery and remove the strings, if necessary. Cut the stalks into small pieces. Add the vegetables to the saucepan for the last 30 minutes of cooking and cook until soft. Season the ragout with salt and pepper.

Stir through the flour paste if needed to thicken the gravy, simmering for a further 1–2 minutes to incorporate, then serve.

Forest berry
custard Danish

Makes 6 Danishes

INGREDIENTS

250 g (9 oz) quark or cream cheese
40 g (1½ oz/⅓ cup) icing
  (confectioners') sugar
40 g (1½ oz) vanilla custard powder
3 sheets puff pastry (500 g/1 lb 2 oz)

Also:

1 egg yolk for brushing
250 g (9 oz) mixed forest berries
  (e.g. raspberries, strawberries,
  blueberries)
Icing (confectioners') sugar
  for dusting

Preheat the oven to 190°C (375°F). Line a baking tray with baking paper. Whisk the cream cheese with the icing sugar and vanilla custard powder in a bowl.

Divide the pastry into 6 equal portions. Whisk the egg yolk in a small bowl. Brush the edges of the pastry with the egg yolk and place 1 tbsp of the cream cheese mixture in the center of each piece of pastry. Fold the pastry corners towards the center to enclose the filling, either from two opposite, or from all four corners. Transfer the pastry pockets to the baking tray. Brush the tops with the remaining egg yolk.

Bake the Danishes in the preheated oven (bottom rack) until golden, about 20 minutes. Meanwhile, pick through the forest berries. Rinse carefully if necessary, pat dry, and clean. Halve any larger berries.

Remove the Danishes from the oven. Leave to cool and divide among plates. Garnish with the berries. Dust with icing sugar and serve.

Baked apples with chestnuts, honey, and hazelnuts

Serves 4

INGREDIENTS

4 tart apples
50 g (1¾ oz/½ cup) hazelnuts
100 g (3½ oz) precooked chestnuts
2 tbsp honey
1 tbsp butter, softened
3 tbsp cranberries (from a jar)

Also:
1 orange
1 lemon
50 g (1¾ oz) honey
250 ml (9 fl oz/1 cup) white wine

Preheat the oven to 200°C (400°F). Wash the apples. Use an apple corer to remove the cores, then place the apples upright inside a small roasting dish.

Coarsely chop the hazelnuts and dry-roast them in a frying pan until golden brown. Leave the nuts to cool slightly, then chop finely and combine with the chestnuts, honey, butter, and cranberries in a bowl. Stuff the apple cores with the nut mixture.

Wash the orange and lemon under hot water, pat dry, and slice. Stir the honey into the white wine and pour the liquid around the apples. Add the sliced orange and lemon to the dish.

Cook the apples in the preheated oven (bottom rack) for 30–35 minutes. Divide them among plates while still warm and serve.

Mini red wine cupcakes with a cheesecake heart

Makes 10 cupcakes

INGREDIENTS

For the batter:
110 g (3 ¾ oz) dark chocolate
150 g (5 ½ oz) butter, softened
50 g (1 ¾ oz) icing (confectioners')
  sugar
Salt
½ tsp vanilla extract
3 eggs
1 orange
60 g (2 ¼ oz) caster (superfine)
  sugar
100 ml (3 ½ fl oz) red wine
170 g (6 oz) plain (all-purpose) flour
2 pinches baking powder
100 g (3 ½ oz) ground hazelnuts

For the cheesecake hearts:
250 g (9 oz) quark or cream cheese
1 egg yolk
1 pinch salt
20 g (¾ oz) vanilla custard powder
50 g (1 ¾ oz) icing (confectioners')
  sugar

For the topping:
150 g (5 ½ oz) mascarpone
150 ml (5 fl oz) heavy cream
40 g (1 ½ oz/⅓ cup) icing
  (confectioners') sugar

Also:
200 g (7 oz) redcurrants or blueberries
Icing (confectioners') sugar for dusting
  (to taste)

For the batter, finely chop the chocolate. Transfer to a small bowl and carefully melt over a double boiler, stirring constantly. Set aside to cool briefly. Add the butter, icing sugar, salt, and vanilla and whisk until foamy.

Separate the eggs. Whisk the egg yolks into the batter mixture one by one. Wash the orange under hot water, pat dry, and finely grate the zest. Stir the zest into the batter. Whisk the egg whites until semi-stiff, gradually adding the sugar. Continue to whisk until the mixture is creamy. Fold the egg whites into the chocolate mixture, then carefully stir in the red wine. Sift the flour and baking powder together. Fold into the batter together with the nuts.

Preheat the oven to 170°C (325°F). For the cheesecake heart, whisk the cream cheese, egg yolk, salt, vanilla custard powder, and icing sugar until well combined. Transfer the mixture to a piping bag with a round nozzle (about 5 mm/¼ inch). Place 10 strong paper muffin cups, or silicone cups (6 cm/2½ inches in diameter) onto a baking tray and fill to about three quarters with the chocolate batter. Gently press the nozzle of the piping bag into the center of the batter and pipe a little of the cheesecake into the batter. Bake the cupcakes in the preheated oven (bottom rack) for 25–30 minutes, then set aside to cool.

For the topping, combine all the ingredients and whisk until creamy. Transfer to a piping bag. Garnish the cooled red wine cupcakes with the topping. Wash and pat dry the redcurrants and pick them off their stems. Garnish the cupcakes with the redcurrants. Serve dusted with icing sugar to taste.

The Little
Mermaid

ar out in the sea, the water is as blue as the petals of the most stunning corn-flower and as clear as the purest glass. But it is also very deep, deeper than any anchor rope will go. That is where the merpeople live.

Their realm is home to the strangest of trees and plants, which are so supple that they move with the slightest stir in the water as though they were alive. Fish dart in and out of the branches like the birds flit through the trees on land. At the deepest point in the sea rises the palace of the king of the merpeople. The palace walls are made of coral, and its tall, pointed windows of the clearest amber. The roof is formed by mussel shells that open and close depending on how the water flows, and each shell holds sparkling pearls.

The king of the merpeople had been a wid-ower for many years, and his children, the little mermaid princesses, were looked after by his old mother. All six of the king's children were very pretty, but the youngest was the most beautiful of them all. Her skin was as fine and clear as a rose petal, her eyes were as blue as the deepest sea but, like all the others, she did not have feet. Instead, she had a fish tail.

Her greatest joy was to hear about the world of the humans. Her grandmother knew every-thing about ships and cities, people and animals. What seemed most wonderful to the little mermaid was that up on land, flowers had a scent, because those at the bottom of the sea did not, that forests were green and that the 'fish' flitting about between the trees could sing loudly and sweetly.

'When you turn fifteen,' said the grandmother, 'you'll be allowed to swim up to the surface from the bottom of the sea, to sit on the rocks in the moonlight and to watch the big ships sailing by.' The following year, the first of the sisters would turn fifteen, and she promised the others that she would tell them about everything she would discover.

None of them waited more eagerly than the youngest. Many a night she stood by her open window, looking up through the dark blue water, watching the fish wave their fins and flick their tails.

Finally the oldest princess had her fifteenth birthday and was allowed to rise up to the surface of the sea. When she returned, she had lots to tell her sisters, but the most beautiful thing of all, she said, was to lie on a sand bar in the moonlight, gazing at the nearby coast and city, whose lights twinkled like hundreds of stars.

The next year, the second sister was given permission to rise up to the surface and to swim wherever she wanted. She came up just as the sun was setting, and she thought that this was the most magnificent of all the sights she saw. She said that the entire sky had looked like liquid gold, and words failed her when she tried to describe the beauty of the clouds.

The following year, it was the third sister's turn. She was the boldest of them all and swam up a broad river that flowed into the sea. She saw gloriously green hills full of vineyards and glimpsed palaces and castles in splendid woods.

The fourth sister was less bold. She stayed out in the wild sea and told her sisters that this was the most wondrous place. You could see all around you for miles and miles, and the sky above you was like a dome of glass.

The year after, it was the fifth sister's turn. Her birthday was in winter, and so she saw things none of the others had seen the first time they ventured to the surface. The sea looked a deep green, and there were large icebergs drift-ing about, each one shimmering like a pearl, she said.

Each of the sisters was delighted about all the new and beautiful sights they discovered on the surface during their first outing. But as they grew up and were allowed to rise to the surface any time they wanted, they no longer cared much about it. Instead, they longed to return to their world at the bottom of the sea. But the youngest sister was so sad with longing that she wanted to weep. However, mermaids have no tears and therefore suffer even more. 'Oh, how I wish I was fifteen already!' she said. 'I know that I'll care very much about the world up there and the people who live in it.'

Finally her fifteenth birthday came. 'Now you're grown up!' said the grandmother. 'Come, I'll adorn you like your sisters.' She put a wreath of white lilies into the little mermaid's hair, and each of the petals was formed from half a pearl. 'Goodbye,' the little mermaid said, and up she swam, as light and effortless as a bubble of air.

The sun had just set when she raised her head up above the water, but the clouds were still glowing like gold and roses and the evening star sparkled bright and clear in the pale red sky. The air was mild and fresh, and the sea calm. There was a large three-master sailing ship ahead of her. There was music and singing, and as night fell, hundreds of colorful lanterns were lit all over the ship.

The little mermaid swam to the window of a cabin, where she saw a young prince, the handsomest of all the people on board. He had big dark eyes and was celebrating his sixteenth birthday on the ship. The sailors danced on deck, and when the young prince stepped out, a hundred or more colorful rockets were launched into the sky. This frightened the little mermaid, and she dived down below. When she peeped up again a little later, it seemed to her as if all of the stars in the sky were raining down upon her. She

> **'I know that I'll care very much about the world up there and the people who live in it.'**

hardly believed her eyes, as she had never seen anything like it.

It got very late, but the mermaid could not take her eyes off the ship and the handsome prince. However, deep down in the sea the water began to rumble and roar. The ship started to pick up more and more speed, and the waves grew larger and larger. Great clouds gathered in the sky, and lightning flashed in the distance. The ship pitched and rolled in the wild sea where the waves rose like black mountains. It creaked and cracked, and its thick planks bent with the heavy blows of the waves breaking over its deck and on its sides. The mast snapped in two, and the ship listed over to its side while the water streamed into the hull. The mermaid realized that the seamen were in danger. For a moment, everything was pitch-black, but then, in a bright flash of lightning, she saw the young prince sink down into the deep sea. The little mermaid fought her way through the storm and reached him just as his arms and legs threatened to give. He would have died had she not come to his rescue. She held his head above the water and let the waves take both of them wherever they wanted.

In the morning, the storm had passed, and the sun rose bright and red from the water. But the prince's eyes remained closed. The mermaid kissed his forehead and pushed his wet hair out of his face. Ahead, she saw dry land with tall mountains whose peaks glistened with snow. Down by the coast, there were magnificent green woods, and in the foreground there was a temple, where the sea formed a little bay. This is where she swam with the prince and laid him down on the sand. Suddenly, a number of young girls came into the garden. The little mermaid swam further out, behind some tall rocks that stuck out of the water. She covered her hair with sea foam so that nobody would be able to see her little face. This is how she watched to see who would come to find the poor prince.

It didn't take long before one of the young girls saw the prince. At first, she seemed frightened, but only for a moment. The little mermaid watched as the prince regained consciousness and smiled at the girl. But he didn't smile at the mermaid – after all, he did not know that she had saved him. She felt very sad, and when she saw him being led inside the large building, she dived

down unhappily into the water and returned to her father's palace.

She had always been quiet and contemplative, but now became much more so. Her sisters asked her what she had seen on her first visit to the surface, but she did not tell them a thing.

Many evenings and mornings she swam up to the spot where she had left the prince behind. She watched the fruits in the garden ripen and be picked, and she saw the snow melt on the tall mountains, but she never saw the prince again, so each time she returned home a little sadder than when she had left. Finally, she could not bear it any longer and told one of her sisters what had happened. Then the other sisters heard about it, who told their friends. One of them knew who the prince was and where his kingdom could be found. 'Come, little sister!' said the other princesses, and arm in arm they swam up to the surface and to the prince's palace.

Now that the little mermaid knew where he lived, she visited every evening and every night. She swam much closer to the shore than any of her sisters would have dared, and there she stayed and watched the young prince. Some evenings, she would see him sail out to sea on his splendid ship, with music playing on board.

On many nights, when the fishermen were out at sea with their torches, she heard them say many good things about the young prince, and she was happy that she had saved his life. She grew to like humans more and more, and more and more she longed to live among them, because their world seemed to be so much wider than her own. There was so much that she wanted to know, and because her sisters did not know all the answers to her questions she asked her grandmother, who knew the world above the sea well. 'If people don't drown,' the little mermaid asked, 'do they then live forever? Don't they die like we do here under the sea?'

'Yes,' said her grandmother, 'they too must die, and their lifespan is even shorter than ours.

We can live to be three hundred years, and when we pass away, we are only turned into foam on the water. We have no immortal soul, and we never regain life. Humans, in contrast, have a soul that lives forever, even after their bodies have turned to dust.'

'Why don't we have an immortal soul?' asked the little mermaid sadly. 'I'd gladly give the hundreds of years that I still have ahead of me just to be human for a day.' 'You must not think like that!' said the old woman. 'We are much happier and better off here than the humans in the world above.' 'So I will die and drift as foam across the sea, neither hearing the music of the waves nor seeing the beautiful flowers or the red sun? Can't I do anything to gain an immortal soul?'

'No,' answered her grandmother. 'Only if a human loved you so much that you meant more to him than his father and mother, if all of his thoughts and all of his love were dedicated to you and he promised to be faithful to you for all eternity, then his soul would flow over into your body and you would also share in the happiness of humans. He would give his soul to you and yet keep his own. But that can never happen. What we think is beautiful here under the sea – your fish tail – is considered ugly on land. There, you need two ungainly props they call legs to be thought beautiful.'

The little mermaid sighed and looked unhappily at her fish tail. She thought to herself, *I'd gladly risk everything to win him and an immortal soul! I'll go visit the sea witch, of whom I have always been so afraid. Perhaps she will be able to help*. The little mermaid left her garden and swam out past the roaring whirlpools where the sea witch lived. There stood the witch's house, in the midst of a strange forest surrounded by polyps. Terrified, the little mermaid stopped. Her heart beat wildly with fear, and she almost turned back, but the thought of the prince and the human soul gave her courage.

Finally, she reached a large, swampy clearing in the forest with fat water snakes coiled everywhere. In the middle of the clearing was a house built of the bones of shipwrecked people, and there sat the sea witch. 'I already know what you want,' said the witch. 'It is foolish of you, yet you shall have your way, even though it will bring you nothing but grief, my beautiful princess. You want to lose your fish tail so that the young prince will fall in love with you and you can win an immortal soul!' said the witch with a horrendous cackle. 'I'll make you a potion. Before sunrise, you must swim to the shore with it, sit down on dry land, and drink the potion. Your tail will disappear and shrink to form what humans call legs. But this will hurt; it will feel as if a sharp sword cut you in two. Everyone who sees you will say that you are the most beautiful human being they have ever seen. You will retain your weightless movement, but every step you take will be as if you are treading on sharp knives, as if your blood must surely flow. But remember,' said the witch, 'once you have taken a human form, you can never be a mermaid again! You will not be able to return to the sea, to your sisters and your father's palace. And if you fail to win the prince's love, you will not gain an immortal soul. The first morning after he marries another, your heart will break, and you will turn into foam on the sea.' 'I will do it,' said the little mermaid, turning as pale as death.

'Can't I do anything to gain an immortal soul?'

'But you also need to pay me,' said the witch, 'and I ask a steep price. You have the sweetest voice of all down here at the bottom of the sea. Surely you hope to enchant the prince with it, but it is your voice you must give to me. The best you have is what I want in exchange for my precious potion!' 'But if you take my voice away from me,' said the little mermaid, 'what will I have left?' 'Your lovely form,' said the witch, 'your weightless motion and your eloquent eyes. All these will serve you well in enchanting a human heart. Or have you lost courage? Stick out your little tongue, and I shall cut it off. I'll have my payment, and you'll get your powerful potion.' 'So be it,' said the little mermaid.

The sun had not yet risen when she reached the prince's palace. The little mermaid drank the fiery potion, and it was as if a two-edged sword sliced through her body. She fainted. When the sun rose above the sea, she awoke and felt a searing pain. But directly in front of her stood the handsome prince. She cast down her eyes and saw that her fish tail had gone. Instead, she had the loveliest pair of legs a girl could hope to have. But she was naked, so she covered herself with her own hair. The prince asked her who she was and how she came to be there. She looked at him sadly with her deep blue eyes, for she could not speak. So he took her by his hand and led her inside the castle. Each step felt as if she was treading on sharp needles and knives, but she happily bore the pain, gliding along on the prince's hand as lightly as a bubble.

The little mermaid charmed everybody, especially the prince, who called her his little foundling. She grew more dear to the prince with each day that went by, and he loved her like one loves a good child, but he never thought of making her his queen. 'Don't you love me best of all?' the little mermaid's eyes seemed to ask whenever he took her into his arms. 'Yes, you are dearest to me,' said the prince, 'because you have the kindest heart of all. And you remind me of a young girl I once saw but surely shall never find again. I was on a ship that was wrecked. The waves cast me ashore near a holy temple, where a girl rescued me. I only saw her twice. She would be the only one I could ever love, but you are so like her that you almost replace her memory in my thoughts. She belongs to the temple, so my good fortune sent you across my path.' 'Alas, he does not know that it was me who saved his life,' thought the little mermaid.

One day, it was announced that the prince was to marry the beautiful daughter of a neighboring king. 'I must travel,' he said to the little mermaid 'to meet the beautiful princess. This is my parents' wish, but they cannot force me to bring her home as my bride. I cannot love her! She does not resemble the lovely girl from the temple.'

Next morning, the ship sailed into the neighboring king's harbor. The princess was not there yet. People said that she was being educated at a holy temple far, far away, where she was taught every royal virtue. Finally the princess arrived. The little mermaid was curious to see how beautiful the princess would be, and she had to admit that she had never seen anyone more exquisite than her. The princess's skin was clear and fair, and her smiling dark blue eyes were veiled by long, dark lashes.

'It is you who rescued me when I was lying on the shore, half dead!' exclaimed the prince and took his wife into his arms. 'Oh, I am happy

> 'Yes, you are dearest to me,' said the prince, 'because you have the kindest heart of all.'

beyond words!' he said to the little mermaid. 'My fondest dream has come true, which I never dared hope for. You are sure to share my joy, for you love me more than anyone else.' The little mermaid kissed his hand, but inside she felt as if her heart was breaking.

On the day of the wedding, the bride and groom joined their hands, and their marriage was blessed. The little mermaid was clothed in silk and gold and held the bride's train, but her ears did not hear the festive music, nor did her eyes take in the wedding ceremony. She only thought of the night ahead, when she would die, and of everything she had lost in this world.

That same evening, the wedded couple went aboard the ship. When night fell, colorful lanterns were lit, and the seamen danced merrily on deck. The little mermaid remembered the first time she rose from the sea, when she had first watched such a joyful, sumptuous celebration. She joined in the dance, floating above the deck. Everyone cheered her – never before had she danced so wonderfully. Every step was like a sharp dagger cutting into her tender feet, yet she did not feel a thing, because there was a much sharper pain in her heart. She knew this would be the last evening that she would ever see him. The prince kissed his lovely bride, and hand in hand they went to their magnificent tent on deck.

The little mermaid rested her arms on the ship's rail and looked to the east. There she saw her sisters rise from the waves; they were pale, and their long hair no longer blew in the wind. It had all been cut off. 'We gave it to the witch so that we could help you. She gave us a knife, see how sharp it is? Before the sun rises, you must thrust it into the prince's heart, and when his warm blood spatters on your feet, they will again grow together and form a fish tail, and you will become a mermaid again. Come back to us! Hurry!'

The little mermaid went to the tent, where she saw the beautiful bride resting her head on the prince's chest. She kissed his forehead and saw the sky reddening before dawn. She looked at the sharp knife and threw it far out into the sea. Once more, she looked at the prince, with her eyes already glazing, before hurling herself down into the sea, where she felt her body dissolve in the foam.

When she looked up, she saw the bright sun, and above her there were hundreds of exquisite, ethereal creatures floating in the sky without wings, as they were as light as the air itself. The little mermaid realized that she now had a body just like these beings, and that she was gradually rising from the foam.

'Where am I going?' she asked, and her voice sounded like that of the other creatures, so other-worldly that it was clearly no earthly music. 'To join the daughters of the air!' they answered. 'The daughters of the air have no immortal soul, but they can earn one through good deeds. We spread the scent of the flowers and carry joy and healing wherever we go. When we have tried to do as much good as we can for three hundred years, we are given an immortal soul. You, poor little mermaid, have strived for the same thing as we with your whole heart; you have suffered and have now risen to join the spirits of the air. By doing good, you can now earn yourself an immortal soul.'

The little mermaid lifted her sorrowful eyes towards the sun, and for the first time her eyes were wet with tears. Down on board the ship, she saw the prince and his beautiful bride search for her. Invisibly, she kissed the bride's forehead, smiled at the prince, and floated up to the rose-red clouds together with the other daughters of the air.

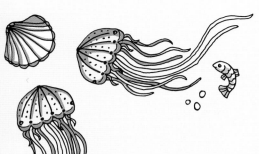

A day by the seaside

Just as the little mermaid was enticed to join the handsome prince on land, we're happy to be enchanted by the culinary offerings of the sea. This is where maritime freshness marries summery, light flavors – welcome to the mysterious world below the sea!

APPETIZER

Vegetarian miso soup
with wakame and egg

MAIN COURSE

Lemon spaghetti
with clams

DESSERT

Salted caramel
parfait

Prawns on toasted crusty bread with lemon mayonnaise

Serves 4

INGREDIENTS

For the lemon mayonnaise:
1 egg yolk
1 tbsp dijon mustard
½ tsp salt
1 lemon
50 ml (1½ fl oz) olive oil
60 ml (2 fl oz/¼ cup)
  sunflower oil

For the prawns:
1 lemon
3 dill sprigs
600 g (1 lb 5 oz) prawns
  (shrimp) (pre-cooked)
3 tbsp olive oil
Salt
Freshly ground black pepper

Also:
2 tbsp olive oil
8 slices crusty white bread
  (e.g. baguette)
Organic, edible flowers
  for garnish

For the lemon mayonnaise, combine the egg yolk, mustard, and salt in a tall container. Halve and juice the lemon. Add the lemon juice to the mixture. Blend everything for about 1 minute with a hand-held blender, then slowly drizzle in the olive oil and sunflower oil. Continue to blend until you have a creamy mayonnaise.

For the prawns, wash the lemon under hot water, pat dry, and finely grate the zest. Halve and juice the lemon. Rinse the dill, shake off any excess water, pick off the leaves, and chop finely. Toss the prawns with the olive oil, lemon juice and zest, and season with salt and pepper. Stir in the dill.

Heat the olive oil in a frying pan. Add the bread slices and toast until crunchy and golden on both sides. Divide the toast, prawns, and lemon mayonnaise among plates. Garnish with edible flowers and serve.

Roasted tomatoes
with seaweed salad

Serves 4

INGREDIENTS

For the tomatoes:
4 oxheart (beefsteak) tomatoes
3 tbsp olive oil
Sea salt
Freshly ground black pepper
1 tbsp sugar

For the goat's cheese cream:
1 lemon
140 g (5 oz) soft goat's cheese
Salt
Freshly ground black pepper

For the seaweed salad:
2 tbsp olive oil
1 tbsp red wine vinegar
Sea salt
60 g (2¼ oz) samphire

Also:
8 thin slices bread

For the tomatoes, preheat the oven to 180°C (350°F). Wash the oxheart tomatoes, pat them dry, and transfer to a small roasting dish. Brush with olive oil and sprinkle with a little sea salt, pepper, and the sugar. Roast the tomatoes in the preheated oven (bottom rack) for about 20 minutes. After about 10 minutes, place the slices of bread on the oven rack next to the roasting dish and toast until golden brown.

For the goat's cheese cream, wash the lemon under hot water, pat dry, and finely grate the zest. Halve and juice the lemon. Reserve the juice for the seaweed salad. Combine the soft goat's cheese with salt, pepper, and the lemon zest.

For the seaweed salad, whisk the olive oil, red wine vinegar, reserved lemon juice, and a little sea salt in a bowl. Toss with the samphire.

Arrange the warm tomatoes on the goat's cheese cream and serve together with the seaweed salad and toasted bread.

Vegetarian miso soup with wakame and egg

Serves 4

INGREDIENTS

1 leaf dried wakame seaweed
  (from Asian or health food stores)
2 spring onions (scallions)
150 g (5½ oz) tofu
1 lime
4 eggs
700 ml (24 fl oz) vegetable stock
2 tbsp white miso paste
3 tbsp soy sauce

Soak the wakame in a bowl of hot water for about 20 minutes. Wash and trim the spring onions and thinly slice them diagonally. Finely dice the tofu. Halve and juice the lime.

Cook the eggs in a saucepan of boiling water until just set, about 7 minutes. Drain the eggs. Run them under cold water, then peel and halve lengthways.

Briefly bring the vegetable stock to a boil. Reduce the heat and stir in the miso paste, soy sauce, lime juice, and tofu. Don't let the soup return to a boil. Thinly slice the wakame seaweed and add it to the soup.

Divide the miso soup among deep plates. Serve garnished with the halved eggs and spring onion.

Marinated trout
with beetroot

Serves 4

INGREDIENTS

½ small orange
½ small lemon
1 bunch dill
1 tsp fennel seeds
1 tsp juniper berries
2 tbsp sugar
10 g (¼ oz) sea salt
100 g (3½ oz) beetroot (beets)
4 fresh trout fillets

Also:
1 lemon
1 punnet cress or alfalfa sprouts
1 baguette
2 tbsp olive oil
2 tbsp mayonnaise
Organic, edible flowers
  for garnish
Sea salt for sprinkling

Wash the orange and lemon halves under hot water, pat dry, and slice thinly. Rinse the dill, shake dry, and chop coarsely. Coarsely grind the fennel seeds and juniper berries in a mortar and pestle, then combine with the sugar, sea salt, and dill. Peel and coarsely grate the beetroot – this is best done wearing disposable gloves. Combine the grated beetroot with the spices.

Debone the trout fillets and arrange them in a single layer in a large, shallow dish. Drizzle evenly with the marinade and top with the orange and lemon slices. Cover the dish with plastic wrap and leave the fish fillets to marinate in the refrigerator for 12 hours. Remove the fillets from the marinade and cut them into thin slices.

Wash the lemon under hot water, pat dry, and slice. Cut the cress, rinse, and shake dry. Slice the baguette diagonally. Heat the olive oil in a frying pan, add the bread slices, and toast until golden on both sides. Divide the sliced fish fillets among the bread slices. Garnish with mayonnaise, cress or alfalfa sprouts, lemon slices, and edible flowers. Serve sprinkled with sea salt.

Mackerel salad with a tomato medley

Serves 4

INGREDIENTS

For the salad:
600 g (1 lb 5 oz) assorted tomatoes
3 spring onions (scallions)
4 mackerel fillets
  (about 100 g/3½ oz each)
Salt
Freshly ground black pepper
2 tbsp olive oil
1 tsp coriander seeds
1 tbsp butter

For the marinade:
3 tbsp olive oil
2 tbsp white balsamic vinegar
1 tsp sugar
Salt
Freshly ground black pepper
1 tsp dijon mustard

Also:
½ bunch basil
Sea salt for sprinkling

For the salad, wash the tomatoes. Remove the stems and slice. Wash and trim the spring onions and thinly slice them diagonally.

For the marinade, combine the olive oil, white balsamic vinegar, sugar, salt, pepper, and mustard. Divide the sliced tomatoes among plates and drizzle with the marinade.

Season the mackerel fillets with salt and pepper. Heat the olive oil in a frying pan and fry the mackerel fillets for a few minutes on each side. Coarsely grind the coriander seeds in a mortar and pestle. Add to the pan together with the butter and continue to fry briefly. Use a spoon to baste the mackerel fillets a few times with the melted butter.

Rinse the basil, shake dry, and pick off the leaves. Arrange the mackerel fillets on top of the tomatoes. Sprinkle with sea salt and serve garnished with the spring onion and basil.

Cod in a white wine sauce with capers

Serves 4

INGREDIENTS

For the tomatoes:

300 g (10½ oz) assorted tomatoes
2 tbsp olive oil
Salt
1 pinch sugar
1 garlic clove
1 rosemary sprig

For the white wine sauce:

1 onion
2 garlic cloves
1 tbsp butter
100 ml (3½ fl oz) white wine
100 ml (3½ fl oz) vegetable stock
  (or chicken stock)
50 g (1¾ oz) cream cheese
50 ml (1½ fl oz) heavy cream
Salt
Freshly ground pepper

For the capers:

100 ml (3½ fl oz) sunflower oil
1 tbsp capers in sea salt (from a jar)

For the cod:

4 cod fillets (about 150 g/
  5½ oz each)
Salt
Freshly ground pepper
2 tbsp flour
2 tbsp olive oil
1 garlic clove
2 tbsp butter

Preheat the oven to 220°C (425°F). Wash and halve the tomatoes and remove the stems. Scrape out the seeds with a spoon. Transfer the tomato halves to a baking tray. Toss them with the olive oil, salt, and sugar and arrange them in a single layer. Crush the garlic clove (unpeeled) and add to the tomatoes together with the rosemary. Cook the tomatoes in the preheated oven (middle rack) for about 15 minutes.

Meanwhile, peel the onion and garlic for the white wine sauce. Mince the garlic and finely dice the onion. Melt the butter in a small saucepan, add the onion and garlic, and sweat for a few minutes. Deglaze with the white wine. Simmer for about 1 minute to reduce a little, then stir in the vegetable stock, cream cheese, and cream. Continue to simmer for another 3 minutes. Blend until smooth with a hand-held blender and season with salt and pepper.

For the capers, heat the oil to about 170°C (325°F) in a small saucepan. Add the salted capers and deep-fry briefly until crisp. Remove with a slotted spoon and drain on paper towel.

For the cod, season the fish fillets with salt and pepper. Coat in a little flour. Heat the oil in a large frying pan. Add the fish fillets and fry for 2 minutes per side. Crush the garlic clove (unpeeled) and add to the pan together with the butter. Baste the fish repeatedly with the melted butter. Turn off the heat and leave to rest briefly in the pan. Divide the cod among plates together with the tomatoes, white wine sauce, and capers, and serve.

Tip:

If you like, garnish the cod with watercress and serve with mashed potatoes, polenta, or crusty white bread.

Potatoes in a salt crust with dips

Serves 4

<u>**INGREDIENTS**</u>

For the potatoes:
900 g (2 lb) small, waxy
*   potatoes (e.g. Dutch cream)*
2 tbsp sea salt

For the curried dip:
½ lemon
250 g (9 oz) sour cream
1 tbsp mayonnaise
Salt
Freshly ground pepper
1 tbsp curry powder

For the carrot dip:
½ lemon
1 carrot
Salt
125 g (4½ oz) crème fraîche

Also:
1 handful watercress

Thoroughly scrub and clean the potatoes and transfer them to a wide saucepan. Add enough cold water to cover the potatoes half way. Sprinkle with the sea salt. Bring to a gentle simmer and cook, uncovered, for about 15 minutes. Increase the temperature and continue to cook the potatoes for another 10 minutes until they are covered with a dusting of sea salt.

Meanwhile, juice the half lemon for the curried dip. Whisk the sour cream and mayonnaise with a little salt, pepper, the curry powder, and lemon juice in a small bowl.

For the carrot dip, juice the half lemon. Peel and finely grate the carrot. Combine with the lemon juice and season with a little salt. Set the grated carrot aside for 10 minutes, then fold in the crème fraîche.

Rinse the watercress and shake dry. Serve the potatoes together with the dips, garnished with the watercress.

Rainbow trout fillet
with pea purée

Serves 4

INGREDIENTS

For the pea purée:
330 g (11½ oz/2⅓ cups)
   frozen peas
1 garlic clove
1 tbsp olive oil
1 tbsp crème fraîche
Salt
Freshly ground black pepper

For the rainbow trout:
1 lemon
4 garlic cloves
2 stems lemongrass,
   pale part only
1 piece fresh ginger
   (about 3 cm/1¼ inches)
8 thyme sprigs
4 rainbow trout fillets
   (about 170 g/6 oz each)
Salt
Freshly ground black pepper

Also:
Radish sprouts for garnish

For the pea purée, defrost the frozen peas. Peel and mince the garlic. Heat the olive oil in a saucepan. Add the garlic and sweat briefly, then add the peas and crème fraîche. Season with salt and pepper. Bring everything to a boil briefly, then blend until smooth with a hand-held blender. Adjust the seasoning.

For the rainbow trout, preheat the oven to 180°C (350°F). Wash the lemon under hot water and pat dry. Finely peel the zest and cut into very fine matchsticks. Slice the lemon thinly and halve the slices. Peel and mince the garlic. Wash and finely chop the lemongrass. Peel and thinly slice the ginger. Rinse the thyme sprigs and shake off any excess water.

Place each rainbow trout fillet on a separate piece of baking paper. Season with salt and pepper. Top with the lemon slices and zest, garlic, lemongrass, sliced ginger, and thyme sprigs. Fold the baking paper sheets to form parcels and transfer these to a baking tray in a single layer. Cook the fish in the preheated oven (middle rack) until done, about 15 minutes.

Divide the fish fillets and pea purée among plates. Garnish with radish sprouts and a sprinkle of pepper.

Lemon spaghetti
with clams

Serves 4

INGREDIENTS

1 kg (2 lb 4 oz) fresh clams
*   (vongole)*
2 garlic cloves
1 French shallot
1 small red chilli
1 bunch parsley
3 tbsp olive oil
250 ml (9 fl oz/1 cup) white wine
1 bay leaf
Salt
300 g (10½ oz) spaghetti
1 lemon

Also:
Olive oil for drizzling

Thoroughly brush and rinse the clams under running water. Discard any open clams. Peel and thinly slice the garlic and shallot. Wash and halve the chilli, remove any seeds and membranes, and chop finely. Rinse the parsley and shake dry. Pick off and finely chop the leaves.

Heat the olive oil in a saucepan. Add the garlic, chilli, and shallot and sweat. Add the clams and sear over a high heat. Stir in the wine and bay leaf and season everything with salt. Simmer the clams for about 5 minutes.

Meanwhile, bring another pot with plenty of salted water to a boil and cook the spaghetti until al dente. Wash the lemon under hot water and pat dry. Finely peel the zest and cut into very fine matchsticks. Slice the lemon into wedges. Drain the spaghetti in a strainer, then toss with the clams and sauce. Stir in the chopped parsley and lemon zest. Drizzle with olive oil. Arrange the spaghetti and clams on plates and serve with the lemon wedges.

Fried king prawns
with cauliflower and chilli oil

Serves 4

INGREDIENTS

For the cauliflower:
1 large cauliflower (about 750 g/
  1 lb 10 oz)
Salt
80 ml (2½ fl oz/⅓ cup) milk
20 ml (¾ fl oz) heavy cream
20 g (¾ oz) butter
Freshly ground black pepper
1 pinch freshly grated nutmeg
2 tbsp olive oil

For the chilli oil:
1 lemon
1 small red chilli
125 ml (4 fl oz/½ cup) olive oil

For the king prawns:
2 garlic cloves
1 lemon
12 raw, unpeeled king prawns
  (jumbo shrimp)
2 tbsp olive oil
Salt
2 rosemary sprigs

Wash the cauliflower. Remove any leaves and boil whole in a large saucepan of salted water for about 10 minutes. Remove the cauliflower from the pot, drain, and cut off four slices, each about 1 cm (½ inch) thick. Dice the remaining cauliflower. You'll need about 250 g (9 oz).

Transfer the diced cauliflower to a saucepan together with the milk, cream, butter, a generous pinch of salt, a little pepper, and the nutmeg. Bring to a boil and cook until soft, about 12 minutes. Remove the diced cauliflower with a slotted spoon. Transfer to a mixing bowl and add half of the liquid from the saucepan. Blend the cauliflower until smooth with a hand-held blender, gradually adding more of the liquid until you have a creamy purée.

For the chilli oil, wash the lemon under hot water, pat dry, and finely grate the zest. Wash the chilli, remove the stem, and chop or slice thinly. Combine the olive oil with the chilli and lemon zest. Heat the olive oil in a frying pan. Add the four cauliflower slices and fry for about 3 minutes per side. Drizzle with the chilli oil and keep warm.

For the king prawns, peel and thinly slice the garlic. Cut the lemon into wedges. Rinse the prawns and pat dry. Heat the olive oil in a frying pan. Season the prawns with salt and sear on both sides. Add the lemon wedges, garlic, and rosemary sprigs and continue to fry for another 4 minutes.

Arrange the king prawns, cauliflower purée, cauliflower slices, and lemon wedges on plates and serve.

Risotto with smoked salmon and fennel

Serves 4

INGREDIENTS

350 g (12 oz) fennel bulb
Salt
1 lemon
3 French shallots
6 tbsp butter, divided
240 g (8¾ oz) risotto rice
250 ml (9 fl oz/1 cup) white wine
1 liter (35 fl oz/4 cups) hot
  vegetable stock
2 tbsp parmesan cheese,
  finely grated
120 g (4¼ oz) smoked salmon

Remove the outer leaves from the fennel bulb. Pick off the fennel fronds. Wash and pat dry and set aside. Halve the fennel bulb and cut out the core in a wedge shape. Thinly slice the fennel and season with salt. Wash the lemon under hot water, pat dry, and finely grate the zest. Combine the lemon zest with the sliced fennel.

Peel and finely chop the shallots. Melt 2 tbsp of the butter in a saucepan. Add the shallots and sweat until translucent. Stir in the sliced fennel and continue to sweat for a few minutes. Add the rice and fry briefly.

Deglaze everything with the white wine. Simmer until the liquid has been absorbed, then add the hot vegetable stock, ladle by ladle, waiting each time until the rice has again absorbed the liquid. Continue to stir frequently. Simmer the risotto until the rice is al dente. Dice the remaining butter and stir it into the cooked risotto together with the parmesan.

Divide the risotto among serving plates. Sprinkle with the reserved fennel fronds and serve garnished with slices of smoked salmon.

Salted caramel parfait

Makes 1 loaf (about 18–22 cm/ 7–8½ inches long)

Serves 4

INGREDIENTS

For the caramel sauce:
80 g (2¾ oz) sugar
250 ml (9 fl oz/1 cup)
  heavy cream
50 ml (1½ fl oz) milk

For the parfait:
60 g (2¼ oz) sugar
300 ml (10½ fl oz) milk
100 g (3½ oz) white chocolate
5 egg yolks
500 ml (17 fl oz/2 cups)
  heavy cream

Also:
1 ripe mango
1 tsp sea salt

For the caramel sauce, heat the sugar in a large frying pan or wide saucepan (about 30 cm/12 inches in diameter) and allow it to caramelize slowly. Only stir when the sugar takes on too much color. Keep shaking the pan.

Heat the cream and milk separately. Add to the caramel and simmer gently until the caramel has dissolved. Set the sauce aside to cool.

For the parfait, caramelize the sugar using the method described above. Gently warm the milk until lukewarm, then stir into the sugar. Simmer until the sugar has dissolved.

Coarsely chop the chocolate. Place in a bowl over a double boiler and melt slowly over a low heat.

Whisk the egg yolks until foamy in a bowl over a double boiler, making sure that the bowl does not touch the hot water and the egg yolks do not become any hotter than 70°C (150°F). Add the hot caramel and milk mixture and continue to whisk over a low heat for about 1 minute. Pass the egg yolk and caramel mixture through a sieve. Fold in the melted chocolate and leave everything to cool.

Whip the cream until stiff, then fold it into the cooled parfait mixture. Line a loaf tin with baking paper. Transfer half of the parfait mixture to the tin, about 2 cm (¾ inch) deep. Top with half of the caramel sauce, then add the remaining parfait mixture. Cover the tin and freeze the parfait for about 8 hours.

Peel the mango and cut the fruit off the pit. Slice thinly. Cut the parfait into thick slices and garnish with the mango and remaining caramel sauce. Serve sprinkled with sea salt.

Lemon tiramisu

Serves 4

<u>INGREDIENTS</u>

3 eggs
80 g (2¾ oz/⅔ cup) icing
  (confectioners') sugar
3 lemons
500 g (1 lb 2 oz) mascarpone
100 ml (3½ fl oz) limoncello
50 ml (1½ fl oz) orange juice
200 g (7 oz) Savoiardi biscuits
  (lady fingers)

Also:
2 lemons
80 g (2¾ oz) sugar

Separate the eggs. Whisk the egg yolks with half of the icing sugar until thick and creamy. Wash the lemons under hot water, pat dry, and finely grate the zest. Halve and juice the lemons. Add the mascarpone, lemon juice, and zest to the egg yolk mixture and stir until smooth.

Beat the egg whites until semi-stiff. Gradually add the remaining icing sugar to the egg whites and continue to beat until stiff. Fold the egg whites into the mascarpone mixture.

Warm the limoncello and orange juice in a small saucepan. Drizzle the liquid over the Savoiardi biscuits, then layer the biscuits and mascarpone cream in a serving bowl, alternating between the two. Finish with a layer of mascarpone cream. Cover the tiramisu and refrigerate for about 3 hours to allow the flavors to develop.

Wash the lemons under hot water, pat dry, and slice thinly. Bring the sugar and 150 ml (5 fl oz) water to a boil. Add the lemon slices and simmer for a few minutes to soften. Leave to cool in the syrup.

Garnish the tiramisu with the drained lemon slices and serve.

Three healthy smoothies

Makes 1 glass each

INGREDIENTS

For the sea buckthorn and carrot smoothie:
25 g (1 oz) cashews
3 dates (pitted)
125 ml (4 fl oz/½ cup) carrot juice
1 tbsp sea buckthorn juice
  (available from health food stores)
125 ml (4 fl oz/½ cup) coconut water

For the cucumber smoothie:
1 green apple (e.g. Granny Smith)
100 g (3½ oz) cucumber
1 lime
1 handful basil
100 g (3½ oz) green grapes
20 g (¾ oz) honey

For the mango shot:
1 lemon
100 g (3½ oz) mango
70 g (2½ oz) coconut milk

Also:
½ carrot (halved lengthways)
½ baby cucumber (halved lengthways)
1 slice of mango

For the sea buckthorn and carrot smoothie, thoroughly blend all the ingredients in a blender. Wash and peel the carrot half and serve with the smoothie.

For the cucumber smoothie, wash, quarter, and core the apple. Wash and dice the cucumber. Halve and juice the lime. Rinse the basil and wash the grapes. Combine all of the prepared ingredients in a blender together with the honey and blend until smooth. Wash the half baby cucumber, halve again lengthways and serve with the smoothie.

For the mango shot, halve and juice the lemon. Peel the mango, dice the fruit, and blend until smooth together with the coconut milk and lemon juice. Serve the shot garnished with a slice of mango.

Beauty
and The Beast

here once lived a rich merchant who had three sons and three daughters. All of his daughters were extremely pretty, especially the youngest one, and that's why she was called 'Beauty'. However, Beauty was not only prettier than her sisters, but she also had a kinder nature. The two older sisters, in contrast, were full of conceit. Every day they made fun of their younger sister because she spent most of her time reading her schoolbooks instead of going to balls. Several wealthy merchants asked for the sisters' hands in marriage, but the two older ones answered that they would only ever consider marrying a duke or an earl at the very least. Beauty, however, thanked her suitors civilly, explained that she was still too young and wanted to stay with her father for a few more years.

One day the merchant lost all of his fortune, leaving him with nothing but a small country house outside the town. With a heavy heart, he told his children that they would have to live in that house in the future and work as farmers for their living.

His two eldest daughters were appalled at the thought and believed that their suitors would still want to marry them even if they were no longer wealthy. But they were very much mistaken. Only Beauty still had gentlemen asking for her hand because she had such a kind heart. However, Beauty said that she could never leave her father in his misfortune and wanted to help him with his work. She worked hard to do everything that needed to be done. After work, she loved to read, play the piano, or sing to herself while spinning. Her two sisters, in contrast, found their new circumstances unbearably boring. They got out of bed late and spent the day mourning the life they had left behind. 'Just see our youngest sister,' they whispered, 'she is such a simple creature that she is content with this dismal situation.'

One day, the merchant received a letter informing him that a ship holding some of his wares had arrived safely and that he should travel to the port to sell his goods. This news delighted the two older sisters, who believed that their life in penury would finally be over. They asked him to bring back beautiful gowns and ribbons for their hair. Beauty, however, did not ask for anything. 'Why don't you ask me to buy something for you?' her father wanted to know. 'Since you're so kind to think of me,' Beauty replied, 'I ask you to bring me a simple rose.'

The merchant set out to the port, but once he arrived, he had to go to court to receive his wares and, after a great deal of effort, he found himself still just as poor as when he had left. On his return journey, he had to cross a large forest and became lost. It snowed incessantly, and an icy, strong wind blew. When night fell, he saw a bright light at a distance and went on towards it. The light came from a great, brightly illuminated palace.

The merchant hastily made his way towards the palace, but when he entered, he was very surprised to find no one inside. He discovered a log fire in a large hall and a table laid with plenty of delicious foods. He said to himself, 'The master of the house will surely come home soon and will forgive me for having taken this liberty.' When he was no longer able to bear his hunger, he ate and

'I ask you to bring me a simple rose.'

drank from the table. Afterwards, he found a room made up with a comfortable bed. As he was quite fatigued, he decided to go to sleep there.

When he awoke the next morning, he was surprised to find clean clothes instead of his travel-soiled ones. He looked out of the window and was astonished to see the grounds not covered in snow but decorated with flowering arbours making for a delightful sight. Finally he went outside to fetch his horse. As he passed one of the arbours carrying magnificent roses, he remembered Beauty's request and broke off a branch with several rose flowers.

Instantly, there was a frightful noise, and he saw such a horrible Beast coming towards him that he almost fainted. 'You are very ungrateful,' said the Beast to him in a terrifying voice. 'I have saved your life by receiving you into my palace, and in return you steal my roses, which I value more than anything else in the world. You have done wrong and shall die for it.' The merchant fell on his knees and beseeched the Beast: 'Dear lord, please forgive me. I did not believe I would offend anybody by picking a rose for one of my daughters.' 'Don't call me "dear lord",' said the monster, 'I am Beast! I do not like pleasantries and want people to say what they think. So don't think you can move me with your flatteries. But didn't you say you had daughters? I will spare you, but only on the condition that one of your daughters is prepared to come here and die in your place. Do not try to change my mind. Go, and if your daughters refuse to die for you, swear to me that you will return here in three months' time.'

The good merchant did not intend to sacrifice any of his children to this ugly monster and

'You have done wrong and shall die for it.'

therefore swore that he would come back. 'But,' said the Beast, 'I do not want you to leave empty-handed. In the room where you slept you'll find a chest. You may put inside it whatever you wish, and I will have it taken to your house.' So the merchant returned to his room, where he found a large number of gold coins, which he packed inside the chest for his family. He fetched his horse from the stable and set off for his home.

As soon as he saw his children, the merchant burst into tears and told them about the misfortune that had befallen him. The two sisters reproached Beauty severely. 'See what your pride has done!' they said. 'It's your fault that father will have to die, and you don't even shed a single tear!' 'Why should I mourn our father's death?' answered Beauty. 'He won't die. Because the monster is happy to accept one of his daughters in his stead, I will deliver myself up to his fury and will be glad to save our father and prove my love for him.' 'No, dear sister,' said her three brothers, 'you shall not die. It is our duty to find the monster and to kill him or to perish under his claws.' 'There is no hope of destroying him,' the merchant told them, 'his powers are too great. I am very moved by Beauty's kind intentions, but I will not have her walk into her certain death. I am old and only have a short time to live anyway.' 'Dear father,' answered Beauty, 'on no account will you walk to the palace by yourself. You cannot prevent me from following you. I would rather be eaten by the monster than die of sorrow about your death.'

No words could change her mind. Beauty insisted on setting out for the palace herself. Her two sisters were secretly delighted about getting rid of her. Meanwhile, the merchant was so in despair about the thought of losing his daughter that he had entirely forgotten about the chest full of gold. To his surprise, he found it by his bedside. He decided not to tell his children anything about his sudden wealth. He only shared his secret with Beauty, who pleaded with him to use the gold as dowries for her sisters so that they would be able to marry. The goodness of her heart was so great that she forgave both of them heartily for what they had done to her.

So it came that Beauty and her father set off to the palace together, where they arrived towards the evening, seeing the palace brightly illuminated ahead of them. The merchant and his daughter entered the great hall, where they found a richly set table. The father's heart was heavy, and he had no appetite, but Beauty, endeavouring to retain her composure, sat down at the table and passed the bowls to her father. To herself, she thought, *Beast surely wants to fatten me up before eating me, since he feeds me so generously.*

They had hardly finished their meal when they heard a loud noise. Believing that the Beast was coming, the merchant farewelled his daughter in tears. When Beauty saw the monster's terrifying form, she took great fright, but quickly composed herself again, and when Beast asked her whether she had come willingly, she managed to say 'yes'. 'You are very good,' said Beast, 'and I am much obliged to you. You, however, good man, will depart tomorrow, and never think of returning here again. I will see you later, Beauty.' 'I will see you later, Beast,' she replied, and the monster immediately retired to his rooms.

Finally, Beauty and the merchant too went to bed, neither believing that they would even

be able to close their eyes all night, but no sooner had they laid down that they fell into a deep slumber. In her dreams, Beauty saw a lady who told her, 'I am content with the generosity of your heart, Beauty. The good deed of sacrificing your life to save your father's shall not go unrewarded.'

The next day, the father farewelled his daughter, overcome by despair. As soon as he was gone, Beauty sat down in the great hall and began to cry. But because she had so much courage and wisdom, she decided not to spend the few hours she had left bemoaning what she could not change. She thought she might as well have a look around the palace. To her great surprise, she discovered a door on which was written 'Beauty's Apartment'. When she opened it, she was dazzled by the splendour she found inside, but what she noticed most were a large bookcase, a piano and several music books. 'They do not want me to get bored,' she said quietly to herself, opening the bookcase. Inside, she found a book that said in golden letters: 'Speak your wishes, give your commands. You are the queen and mistress here.' 'Alas,' she said with a sigh, 'I wish nothing but to see my poor father and to know how he is doing.' She had only murmured these words to herself, and so it was to her great amazement when she looked at a mirror and saw her home in it, where her father was just arriving in a state of great dejection.

At midday, she found the table again set, and she heard delightful music during her meal, even though she did not see anybody. In the evening, when she was about to sit down to supper, she heard the noise that accompanied Beast as he approached, and she began to tremble. 'Beauty,' said the monster to her, 'will you permit me to sit with you while you eat?' 'You are the master here,' answered Beauty fearfully. 'No,' replied the Beast, 'it is you who is the only mistress here. You only need to command me to leave, and I will go instantly. Tell me, is it not so that you find me very ugly?' 'That is true,' admitted Beauty, 'for I cannot lie. But I believe that you have a good heart.' 'That may be so,' replied the Beast, 'but I am not only ugly, I also lack intelligence and wit. I know very well that I am nothing but a stupid beast.' 'You are not stupid just because you believe yourself not to be wise,' said Beauty. 'A stupid animal would never be capable of having such thoughts.' 'Please eat,' asked the monster, 'and try not to get bored in your home. Everything you see in here is yours.' 'You are very kind,' said Beauty, 'and I admit that I am pleased about your good heart. When I consider that, your deformity seems much less ugly to me.' 'I may have a good heart,' replied the Beast, 'but I still remain a monster.' 'There are plenty of people who are greater monsters than you are,' said Beauty, 'and I prefer you just as you are to those whose human form hides a heart of falseness and ingratitude.' 'If I was eloquent,' answered the Beast, 'I would now make you a great compliment to thank you. But I am a fool, and all I can say is that I am greatly obliged to you.' Beauty was scarcely afraid of the Beast anymore, but she took a deep fright when he asked her, 'Beauty, will you be my wife?' For a while, she was silent, full of fear, because she was afraid that a refusal might arouse the monster's rage. Yet at last she said, trembling, 'No, Beast.' The Beast immediately responded

'There are plenty of people who are greater monsters than you are.'

with such a frightful moan that it seemed to reverberate throughout his palace. He said with a mournful voice, 'Good night then, Beauty,' and left. When Beauty was alone, she felt great compassion for the poor Beast. 'Alas,' she said to herself, 'what a pity that he is so ugly; he is such a good-natured thing.'

Beauty spent three months in the palace, leading a quiet life. Every night, the Beast visited her and talked to her animatedly throughout supper. Every day, Beauty discovered new and good qualities in the monster. Seeing him regularly every day, she had become used to his ugliness. She no longer even feared his visits, but instead awaited them eagerly. There was only one thing that caused Beauty concern. Every night before the Beast left her, he asked her if she would be his wife. And every time she answered 'no', he seemed to despair. One day she said to him, 'I wish I could marry you, but I want to be open with you and not give you any false hopes. I will always like you as a friend; try to be satisfied with this.' 'I must, I guess,' said the Beast, 'and if I am honest with myself, I know that people fear me. Yet I love you very dearly. It makes me so happy that you are content to stay here. Promise me that you will never leave me.' At these words, Beauty became embarrassed. In her mirror, she had seen that her father had become sick with the sorrow over having lost his daughter, and she dearly longed to see him again. 'I would promise to never leave you,' said Beauty, 'but I so wish to see my father again that I will surely pine myself to death if you do not grant me my wish.' 'I'd rather die myself than see you unhappy,' replied the Beast. 'I will send you to your father; you

'I care for you too deeply to be the cause of your death.'

shall stay with him and I will die with the grief of having lost you.' 'No,' said Beauty, weeping. 'I care for you too deeply to be the cause of your death. I promise that I will return in eight days' time.' 'You shall be back home tomorrow morning,' said the Beast, 'but remember your promise. You only need to place your ring on a table before you go to bed, when you wish to return to me. Farewell, Beauty.'

When she awoke the next day, she was at her father's house. He rushed to see her and was beside himself with the joy of seeing his beloved daughter again. Her sisters were sent for and joined them with their husbands. Both had been very unhappy in their marriages. The oldest had married a nobleman, handsome as Love, but so besotted by his own appearance that he paid no attention to anything else from morning to night. The second sister had married a very eloquent man, but he only used his wit to cause strife among all around him.

When the sisters greeted Beauty, they realized enviously that she was dressed elegantly and nobly and was as beautiful as a fresh morning. It was to no avail that Beauty welcomed them with all of the warmth of her heart. It only fuelled their jealousy when Beauty told them how happy she was. Envious, the two sisters ran into the garden and asked each other, 'Why should this little fool be happier than we? Aren't we much more lovable than she is?' 'I have an idea,' said the older, 'let us try to detain her here for more than eight days. The Beast will be full of rage about the broken promise, and he might devour her.' Having decided on this plan, they showed her sister so much affection that Beauty broke out in tears with joy and relief. When the eight days had passed, the sisters pretended to be so distraught about Beauty's imminent departure that Beauty promised to stay a little longer. But she soon remembered the grief that she would cause the poor Beast, and she longed for his company.

On the tenth night, she dreamed that she was in the palace garden, where she found the Beast lying lifeless in the grass, mortally ill and unhappy because of her ingratitude. 'What a wicked person I am,' she said to herself in the morning, 'to disappoint a Beast that loves me so dearly? Is it his fault that he is so ugly and not eloquent? He has a good heart, and that is worth more than anything else. Why ever did I refuse to marry him? Neither a man's beauty nor his wit make a woman happy – that comes from a noble character, virtue, and understanding. And the Beast has all of these valuable qualities. While it is not love that I feel for him, it is friendship, respect, and gratitude.' And with these words, Beauty rose, placed her ring on the table and went back to bed. She fell asleep instantly, and when she awoke, she was overjoyed to find herself back in the Beast's palace. She put on her most beautiful dress to please him. She ran through the palace, calling for the Beast. Having searched everywhere with no success, she remembered her dream and despaired deeply. She hurried to the garden and found the Beast lying unconscious on the ground. She believed him to be dead already. Without hesitation, she threw herself upon him and felt his heart still beating. The Beast opened his eyes and said, 'You forgot the promise you made to me. In my grief, I decided to starve myself to death. But I shall die contentedly because I have the

> 'But I shall die contentedly because I have the happiness to see you again.'

happiness to see you again.' 'No, my dear Beast,' said Beauty, 'You shall not die! You shall live to be my husband. Right here I give you my hand, and I swear that I will be none but yours. I thought I only felt friendship for you, but the pain that I feel now shows me clearly that I cannot live without you.'

No sooner had Beauty spoken these words that she saw the palace illuminated all over with sparkling lights. There were fireworks in the sky, and she heard music. But all that pomp was not enough to keep her attention. She turned her gaze back to her dear Beast. But how great was her surprise! The Beast had vanished, and at her feet she saw a handsome prince, who thanked her for having put an end to his enchantment. She could not help but ask him where Beast was. 'You see him at your feet,' answered the prince. 'An evil fairy put a spell on me to live in this ugly shape of a beast until a beautiful maiden would consent to marrying me. You were the only person in the world who would allow herself to see the good that was in me. And if I now offer you my crown, this will be nowhere near enough to show you the extent of my gratitude.' And Beauty extended her hand to the prince, and he rose. Together, they walked to the palace, where Beauty's father and the entire family awaited them in the great hall. The beautiful lady who had appeared in Beauty's dream had brought them all to the palace.

'Beauty,' said the lady, who was indeed a fairy, 'you have received your reward. You have preferred virtue over beauty and eloquence. You deserve having found a man who unites all of these qualities in himself. As to you,' the fairy continued, addressing Beauty's two sisters, 'I know your hearts very well, including all the wickedness they contain. You shall be turned into statues. But underneath the stone shell surrounding you, you shall retain the ability to think and to feel. You shall stand next to the palace gates, and your punishment shall be to watch your sister's happiness. You will only regain your human form if you are able to admit to your errors. But I am afraid that you may remain statues forever. It is possible to conquer one's own pride, anger, and laziness, but transforming a malicious, envious heart is a rare miracle.' The next moment, at a stroke of the fairy's wand, they were all transported to the prince's kingdom. He married Beauty, and they lived a long life of perfect happiness together, as their union was founded on the force of virtue.

Magical encounters

Fruit and cheese, savory cakes, Beauty and the Beast . . .
The latter would certainly agree that things that seem
to be opposites can be married to form something magical,
given the right circumstances. We'll wait to be surprised
as we sit down to a richly set table.

APPETIZER

Grilled peaches with gorgonzola and hazelnuts

MAIN COURSE

Orange chicken

DESSERT

Basil and lime ice cream

Pikelets with bacon and maple syrup

Serves 4

INGREDIENTS

90 g (3 ¼ oz/⅔ cup) buckwheat flour
30 g (1 oz) plain (all-purpose) flour
1 tsp baking powder
2 eggs
250 ml (9 fl oz/1 cup) buttermilk
1 pinch salt
1 tbsp sugar

Also:
Sunflower oil for frying
16 slices of bacon
100 ml (3 ½ fl oz) maple syrup

Combine the flours and baking powder in a mixing bowl. Separate the eggs. Whisk the buttermilk and egg yolks with the flour mixture. Whisk the egg whites and salt until stiff, gradually adding the sugar. Fold the egg whites into the batter.

Heat a little sunflower oil in a frying pan. To the pan, add 2 tbsp of the batter per pikelet and fry the pikelets over a low heat until golden brown, about 2 minutes per side.

Heat a second frying pan and slowly fry the bacon until crisp. Arrange the pikelets and crisp bacon on plates and serve drizzled with the maple syrup.

Grilled peaches with gorgonzola and hazelnuts

Serves 4

INGREDIENTS

4 ripe peaches
1 lemon
2 tbsp olive oil, divided
2 tbsp honey
40 g (1½ oz/¼ cup) hazelnuts
120 g (4¼ oz) mild gorgonzola
 cheese
2 rosemary sprigs
130 g (4½ oz) rocket (arugula)
1 punnet cress, optional

Preheat the oven to 200°C (400°F). Wash, pat dry, and halve the peaches. Remove the pits. Halve and juice the lemon.

Whisk 1 tbsp olive oil with the honey and lemon juice. Heat 1 tbsp olive oil in a frying pan. Add the peaches and fry for about 2 minutes per side. Transfer the peaches to a casserole dish in a single layer, cut side up, and brush with the marinade. Coarsely chop the hazelnuts. Coarsely crumble the gorgonzola cheese and divide it among the peach halves. Sprinkle with the nuts. Rinse the rosemary and shake dry. Add the sprigs to the dish. Bake the peaches in the preheated oven (middle rack) for about 15 minutes.

Meanwhile, pick through the rocket. Wash and spin or pat dry. Divide the green leaves among plates and drizzle with the peach marinade from the roasting dish. Cut the cress, rinse, and shake dry. Arrange the peaches on top of the rocket, sprinkle with the cress, and serve.

Baked brie
with two chutneys

Makes 4 jars of chutney
(250 ml/9 fl oz each)

<u>INGREDIENTS</u>

For the strawberry chutney:
600 g (1 lb 5 oz) strawberries
150 g (5½ oz) onions
1 piece fresh ginger (about 1 cm/
    ½ inch)
4 black peppercorns
230 g (8½ oz) brown cane sugar
1 small bay leaf
100 ml (3½ fl oz) red wine vinegar
1 cinnamon stick
1 lime
Salt

For the tomato chutney:
3 tomatoes
1 onion
1 garlic clove
1 piece fresh ginger (about 1 cm/
    ½ inch)
100 ml (3½ fl oz) white wine vinegar
1 cinnamon stick
2 cloves
½ tsp salt
1 small red chilli
2 tbsp sugar
60 ml (2 fl oz/¼ cup) sunflower oil
1 tbsp mustard seeds

Also:
1 rosemary sprig
1 brie cheese (about 12 cm/
    4½ inches in diameter)

For the strawberry chutney, wash, trim, and halve the strawberries. Peel the onions and ginger. Thinly slice the onions and mince the ginger. Finely crush the peppercorns in a mortar and pestle.

Transfer the onion and ginger to a small saucepan together with 250 ml (9 fl oz/1 cup) water, the pepper, sugar, and bay leaf. Bring to a simmer and cook until soft, about 5–10 minutes. Add a little more water if needed. Towards the end, allow almost all of the liquid to evaporate. Deglaze the onion mixture with the vinegar. Add the cinnamon and strawberries and bring everything to a brief boil. Halve and juice the lime. Season the chutney with the lime juice and some salt. Remove the cinnamon stick and transfer the hot chutney into sterilized jars. Seal the jars.

For the tomato chutney, score the tomatoes crosswise and scald with boiling water for about 40 seconds. Refresh the tomatoes under cold water, peel off the skins, and cut into wedges. Peel the onion, garlic, and ginger and chop everything finely. Transfer to a small saucepan together with the tomatoes, vinegar, cinnamon, cloves, and salt. Bring everything to a boil over a medium heat, stirring continuously. Wash, halve, and deseed the chilli and chop finely. Stir the sugar, chilli, and a little oil into the mixture and simmer the chutney for 5–8 minutes while stirring continuously.

Heat the remaining oil in a small frying pan. Add the mustard seeds, fry for about 1 minute and stir into the tomato chutney. Continue to simmer for another 8–10 minutes to thicken. Transfer the hot chutney to sterilized jars. Seal and leave to cool.

Preheat the oven to 180°C (350°F). Rinse and shake the rosemary dry. Pick off the leaves. Wrap the rosemary and brie in baking paper. Tie the parcel together with kitchen twine. Place the cheese into the preheated oven (bottom rack) and bake for about 15 minutes to melt slightly. Serve the cheese with the two chutneys.

Bread salad

Serves 4

INGREDIENTS

2 red peppers
1 cucumber
1 bunch parsley
4 garlic cloves
2 red onions
100 g (3 ½ oz) cherry tomatoes
1 small red chilli
5 tbsp olive oil, divided
2 tbsp white wine vinegar
1 tsp dried oregano
Salt
Freshly ground black pepper
400 g (14 oz) crusty white bread
  (e.g. baguette)

Wash and halve the peppers. Deseed, remove any white membranes, and slice into strips. Wash the cucumber, peel if preferred, and dice into 2 cm (¾ inch) cubes. Rinse the parsley, shake dry, and chop the leaves.

Peel the garlic and onions. Slice the onions into thin rings and mince the garlic. Wash and halve the cherry tomatoes. Wash, halve, and deseed the chilli. Chop finely. Combine all of the prepared ingredients with 3 tbsp of the olive oil and the vinegar in a large bowl. Season with oregano, salt, and pepper.

Cut the bread into small, thin slices. Heat the remaining olive oil in a large pan. Add the sliced bread and toast until crisp and golden brown all over. Toss the toasted bread with the salad. Set aside for at least 10 minutes to allow the flavors to develop. Divide among plates and serve.

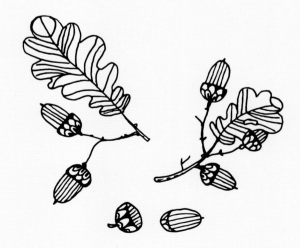

Kohlrabi schnitzels
with pear salsa

Serves 4

INGREDIENTS

For the salsa:
2 firm pears
1 lime
1 red chilli
2 spring onions (scallions)
1 piece fresh ginger
  (about 3 cm/1¼ inches)
3 tbsp olive oil
1 tbsp red wine vinegar
½ tsp salt

For the schnitzels:
4 small kohlrabi
Salt
80 g (2¾ oz) breadcrumbs
80 g (2¾ oz/¾ cup) almond meal
3 eggs
100 g (3½ oz/⅔ cup) plain
  (all-purpose) flour

Also:
500 ml (17 fl oz/2 cups)
  sunflower oil
1 lemon
Sea salt for sprinkling

For the salsa, peel, core, and quarter the pears and dice them into 1 cm (½ inch) cubes. Halve and juice the lime. Wash, halve, and deseed the chilli. Chop finely. Wash, trim, and thinly slice the spring onions. Peel and mince the ginger.

Combine the diced pear with the olive oil, lime juice, red wine vinegar, chilli, spring onion, ginger, and salt in a bowl. Set the salsa aside.

For the schnitzels, peel the kohlrabi and cut them into 1 cm (½ inch) slices. Bring a pot with plenty of salted water to a boil. Add the kohlrabi slices and cook until soft, about 5 minutes. Remove and pat dry.

Combine the breadcrumbs and almond meal in a shallow bowl. Whisk the eggs together in another bowl. Place the flour in a third bowl. Season the kohlrabi slices with salt. Coat them in the flour, then dip them into the eggs, and finally coat them in the breadcrumb mixture.

Heat the sunflower oil to about 180°C (350°F) in a shallow saucepan. Fry the kohlrabi schnitzels in the hot oil until golden brown, about 4 minutes. You may need to do this in batches. Remove the schnitzels with a slotted spoon and drain them on paper towel. Wash the lemon under hot water, pat it dry, halve, and slice it. Arrange the cooked kohlrabi schnitzels on plates together with the salsa and lemon slices. Serve sprinkled with a little sea salt.

Tip:

Serve the kohlrabi schnitzels with a mixed leaf salad.

Tomato and zucchini tarte tatin

Serves 4

**Makes 1 tarte tatin
(24 cm/9½ inches in diameter)**

INGREDIENTS

4 large tomatoes
4 garlic cloves
Salt
4 thyme sprigs
4 tbsp olive oil, divided
1 zucchini
30 g (1 oz) parmesan cheese
1–2 sheets puff pastry
  (about 275 g/9¾ oz)

Also:
1 tbsp pine nuts
1 handful basil leaves
  for garnish

Preheat the oven to 200°C (400°F). Line a baking tray with baking paper. Wash and halve the tomatoes and remove the stems. Scrape out the seeds with a spoon. Arrange the tomato halves on the baking tray. Crush the garlic cloves (unpeeled). Combine the garlic with a little salt, the thyme sprigs, and 2 tbsp olive oil and toss with the halved tomatoes. Roast the tomatoes in the preheated oven (middle rack) for about 30 minutes. Leave the oven on.

Meanwhile, wash, trim, and thinly slice the zucchini. Lightly salt the sliced zucchini, set aside for 10 minutes, then pat dry. Finely grate the parmesan cheese. Heat the remaining olive oil in a frying pan. Add the sliced zucchini and fry for about 2 minutes per side.

Line a 24 cm (9½ inch) round springform cake tin with baking paper. Arrange the fried zucchini and roasted tomatoes, cut side down, evenly across the bottom of the tin. Sprinkle with the parmesan. Cover the vegetables with the puff pastry, folding in any excess dough along the sides of the tin. Bake the tarte tatin in the preheated oven (bottom rack) for about 25 minutes.

Meanwhile, dry-roast the pine nuts in a frying pan until golden brown. Remove the cooked tarte tatin from the oven. Set aside for about 2 minutes, then carefully invert onto a serving board. Serve garnished with the pine nuts and basil leaves.

Potato waffles with cream cheese and red radishes

Serves 4

INGREDIENTS

For the waffles:
400 g (14 oz) floury potatoes
2 eggs
2 tbsp cornflour (cornstarch)
15 g (½ oz) baking powder
60 g (2¼ oz) grated emmental
  cheese
½ tsp salt
Freshly ground black pepper
Freshly grated nutmeg
1 thyme sprig

For the topping:
4 radishes
1 bunch chives
175 g (6 oz) cream cheese
Sea salt
Freshly ground black pepper

Also:
Waffle iron
Sunflower oil

For the waffles, scrub the potatoes and cook them in a saucepan of boiling water for only about 5 minutes. Drain the barely cooked potatoes and set them aside briefly to dry off. Peel and finely grate the potatoes, then combine them with the eggs, cornflour, baking powder, emmental cheese, salt, pepper, and nutmeg. Rinse the thyme and shake dry. Pick off the leaves and stir them into the mixture.

Brush a waffle iron with a little sunflower oil and turn the iron on to heat. Use 3–4 tbsp of the potato mixture per waffle (depending on the size of the waffle iron) and add to the waffle iron. Cook until crisp, about 8 minutes. Repeat until all of the potato batter has been used.

Meanwhile, for the topping, wash and trim the radishes and cut them into thin strips. Rinse the chives, shake off any excess water, and slice thinly. Season the cream cheese with sea salt and pepper and mix until smooth. Divide the warm waffles among plates and top them with the cream cheese, radishes, and chives.

Orange chicken

Serves 4

INGREDIENTS

1 whole kitchen-ready
*   organic chicken*
2 oranges
2 sage sprigs
Salt
2 tbsp orange marmalade
3 small red onions
2 garlic cloves
100 g (3½ oz) truss cherry
*   tomatoes*
2 rosemary sprigs
600 ml (21 fl oz) chicken stock

Also:
Crusty white bread for serving

Rinse the chicken and pat dry. Wash the oranges under hot water, pat dry, and slice thinly. Rinse the sage and shake dry. Slide the sprigs underneath the chicken skin together with 3 orange slices. To make this easier, gently lift the skin off with your fingers to loosen it carefully.

Preheat the oven to 190°C (375°F). Season the chicken with salt and brush it with the marmalade until it is completely coated before transferring it to a roasting dish. Peel and quarter the onions. Crush the garlic cloves in their skin. Rinse the tomatoes and rosemary and pat dry. Add the onions, garlic, tomatoes, rosemary, remaining orange slices, and chicken stock to the roasting dish with the chicken.

Place the orange chicken in the preheated oven (bottom rack) and cook until done, about 50 minutes, basting it throughout with the liquid. If the chicken starts to take on too much color, cover the dish with a sheet of baking paper or foil. Serve with crusty white bread.

Beef fillet salad
with berries

Serves 4

INGREDIENTS

For the dressing:
1 piece fresh ginger
  (about 1 cm/½ inch)
2 garlic cloves
2 tbsp soy sauce
2 tbsp sesame oil
1 tbsp honey
1 tbsp balsamic vinegar
Salt
Freshly ground black pepper

For the salad:
4 small baby eggplants
Salt
3 tbsp olive oil
250 g (9 oz) mixed berries
2 beef fillet steaks
  (about 200 g/7 oz each)
Freshly ground black pepper
150 g (5½ oz) mixed leafy greens

Also:
Radish sprouts for serving
1 tsp sesame seeds

For the dressing, peel and finely mince the ginger and garlic. Combine both with the soy sauce, sesame oil, honey, and balsamic vinegar. Season the dressing with salt and pepper.

For the salad, wash and pat dry the baby eggplants. Halve them lengthways. Score the cut sides of the eggplant crossways and season lightly with salt. Set aside for 5 minutes. Pat the eggplants dry and heat 2 tbsp olive oil in a frying pan. Add the eggplant halves and fry them on all sides for about 3 minutes. Drizzle with a little of the dressing.

Pick through, rinse, and pat dry the berries. Press the steaks gently to flatten them and season with salt and pepper. Heat the remaining olive oil in a frying pan. Add the steaks and fry until pink, about 2 minutes per side. Leave the meat to rest for 5 minutes, then cut it into strips.

Meanwhile, wash and pick through the leafy greens. Dry the greens in a salad spinner, or pat dry, and toss with the dressing before dividing among plates. Arrange the beef fillet strips, eggplants, and berries on top of the salad. Garnish with radish sprouts and sesame seeds.

White pizza
with zucchini

Makes 2 large pizzas

INGREDIENTS

For the pizza dough:
30 g (1 oz) fresh yeast
300 ml (10½ fl oz) lukewarm
  water
1 tsp salt
2 pinches sugar
500 g (1 lb 2 oz/3⅓ cups)
  pizza flour (type 00)

For the topping:
50 g (1¾ oz) parmesan cheese
2 small zucchini
Salt
125 g (4½ oz) crème fraîche
Freshly ground pepper

Also:
Flour for dusting
1 large rosemary sprig
1 tsp pink peppercorns
Olive oil for drizzling

For the dough, crumble the yeast and whisk it into the lukewarm water together with the salt and sugar. Put the flour into a mixing bowl. Add the yeast mixture to the flour and knead everything together for at least 5 minutes with an electric mixer (or 10 minutes by hand). Continue to knead by hand for a few more minutes until the dough is smooth and elastic. Cover the bowl with plastic wrap and leave the dough to rise for about 1 hour.

Meanwhile, finely grate the parmesan for the topping. Wash, trim, and thinly slice the zucchini. Salt the zucchini slices and set them aside for 10 minutes, then pat them dry. Season the crème fraîche with a little salt and pepper and stir to combine.

Preheat the oven to 250°C (500°F). Line two baking trays with baking paper. Dust your benchtop with flour. Halve the dough and roll it out very thinly. Create a slightly thicker edge with your hands. Place one pizza base onto each baking tray. Spread each base with half of the crème fraîche and sprinkle with the grated parmesan cheese. Top evenly with the zucchini slices.

Bake the pizzas in the preheated oven (middle rack), one at a time, for about 15 minutes or until crisp and golden. A few minutes before the pizza is done, rinse and shake dry the rosemary. Pick off the leaves. Sprinkle the pizzas with the rosemary leaves and continue to bake until done. Garnish the pizzas with pink peppercorns and drizzle with olive oil to serve.

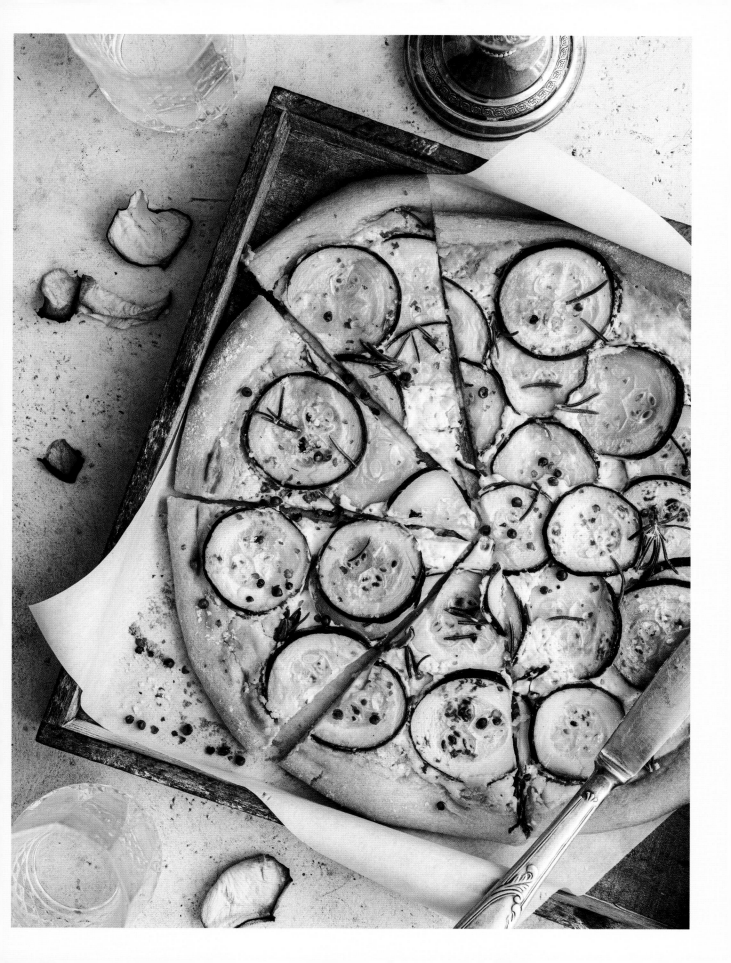

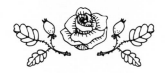

Basil and lime ice cream

Serves 4

INGREDIENTS

4 egg yolks
130 g (4½ oz) sugar
250 ml (9 fl oz/1 cup) milk
250 ml (9 fl oz/1 cup)
  heavy cream
20 g basil leaves
100 ml (3½ fl oz) lime juice

Also:
Ice cream maker
1 pomegranate
1 handful basil leaves
  for garnish

Whisk the egg yolks together with the sugar. Bring the milk and cream to a boil in a small saucepan. Rinse the basil leaves and pat dry. Add the basil to the milk and cream mixture and blend until smooth.

Whisk the egg yolk mixture into the blended liquid until thoroughly combined. Heat everything to a maximum of 80°C (180°F) in a double boiler, whisking continuously until creamy, then strain through a sieve. Stir in the lime juice and keep whisking the mixture until it has cooled down. Transfer to an ice cream maker and leave to freeze.

To serve, halve the pomegranate and remove the seeds. Divide the ice cream into small bowls and serve it garnished with the pomegranate seeds and basil leaves.

Espresso hot chocolate and iced coffee

Serves 4

INGREDIENTS

For the espresso hot chocolate:
400 ml (14 fl oz) milk
100 g (3½ oz) dark chocolate
20 g (¾ oz) unsweetened
  (Dutch) cocoa powder
1 small espresso coffee
  (or 1 tbsp instant
  espresso powder)
200 ml (7 fl oz) heavy cream

For the iced coffee:
600 ml (21 fl oz) milk
1 handful ice cubes
3 tbsp instant coffee powder
3 tbsp icing (confectioners') sugar

Also:
Chocolate shavings for garnish
Unsweetened (Dutch) cocoa powder
  for dusting

For the espresso hot chocolate, bring the milk to a brief boil in a small saucepan. Coarsely chop the chocolate and add it to the milk, together with the cocoa. Stir until the chocolate and cocoa have dissolved, then stir in the espresso.

Whip the cream until stiff. Divide the espresso hot chocolate among cups or mugs and serve garnished with the whipped cream and chocolate shavings.

For the iced coffee, divide the milk and ice cubes among glasses. Add the instant coffee, icing sugar, and 1–2 tbsp water to a small bowl and, using either hand-held electric beaters or a whisk, beat until it forms a thick cream. Use a spoon to top each glass of iced milk with a dollop of coffee cream. Dust the iced coffee with cocoa powder and serve immediately.

Aladdin and
The Magic Lamp

nce upon a time in a large city in the Orient, there lived a tailor who was called Mustapha. He was very poor, and his work hardly earned him enough to feed himself, his wife, or his son, Aladdin.

Aladdin did not care much about his father's work and had no interest in taking up his trade. He preferred to stay out all day in the streets, playing tricks on people together with the other street urchins. Mustapha fell ill with worry about his son's future, soon dying of his grief. Aladdin's mother was forced to sell their shop, and she worked very hard to make a living for the two of them by spinning cotton.

One day, as Aladdin was roaming through the streets, he met a man he had not seen before. The stranger watched the boy for a while before asking Aladdin about his family. He then said that he was in fact Aladdin's uncle and had been living abroad for a long time. But in truth the stranger was a magician from Africa who wanted to use Aladdin for his selfish, wicked plans. Once he had contrived an invitation to Aladdin's home, he impressed both the boy and his mother with his wealth and the generous promise to support his nephew to make him an honest merchant.

He kept his word and introduced Aladdin to the city's most powerful merchants. The mother was immensely grateful for the uncle's generosity and therefore allowed Aladdin to accompany the man to an important meeting outside the city. Aladdin was delighted about this, as he had never been out of the city before. The two of them left, wandering further and further until they finally reached the mountains.

They stopped for the night and lit a fire. When Aladdin asked about the secretive meeting they were to attend, the uncle explained that he needed Aladdin's help in an important matter and that Aladdin might come to see extraordinary things during the course of this business, but that he was not allowed to ask any questions. When the flames of the fire blazed high, the African magician threw in some incense. While Aladdin thought this strange, he trusted the man he believed to be his uncle. Thick smoke rose to the sky, and the magician murmured a series of spells. Suddenly, the earth shook and opened right next to where the magician and Aladdin were standing. A stone appeared with a brass ring fixed to it in the middle. The magician said, 'Below this stone you see in front of you there is a hidden treasure that is destined for you and will make you richer than the richest kings on earth. There is nobody else in the world but you who is permitted to touch or lift this stone. That's why you need to follow my commands. This matter is of the utmost importance for both you and me.' He continued, 'Down there is a cave, where you will find a golden lamp. I ask you to bring me that very lamp.'

They lifted the stone, and Aladdin did what the African magician had commanded him to do. He climbed down and could hardly believe his eyes. He stood in the middle of a treasure chamber, filled to the seams with the most magnificent jewelery, gold and silver, and sparkling precious stones. The boy quickly filled his pockets with these riches and finally found the old, dull oil

> 'Below this stone you see in front of you there is a hidden treasure that is destined for you and will make you richer than the richest kings on earth.'

lamp the uncle had asked him to fetch. But when he climbed up to the surface, holding the lamp, the magician demanded that Aladdin hand him the lamp before leaving the cave himself. Aladdin sensed that something was not right and refused to hand over the lamp. The magician flew into a fitful rage and shouted, 'I'll punish you by leaving you in the cave!' He pushed the stone back to seal the entrance but did not notice that his ring slid off his finger and fell inside the cave.

Aladdin, left behind by himself in the cave, was beside himself with fear. He did not know what to do but was lucky enough to brush against the ring with his foot. Lost in thoughts, he slid the ring onto his finger and began to rub it. Suddenly a large cloud of smoke billowed in front of him, from which emerged an enormous genie of frightful appearance, so tall that he reached from the cave's floor to its ceiling. In a thundering voice, he asked, 'What is your command? Here I am, ready to obey you as your servant and as a servant to those who have the ring on their finger, both I and all other servants of the ring.' Aladdin was terribly frightened, but given his distress he answered without hesitation, 'Whoever you may be, take me away from this place.' No sooner had he spoken these words that the ground opened, and he found himself outside the cave again, at precisely the place where the magician had led him.

Aladdin blinked in the bright daylight and could hardly believe his luck. When he looked around, he recognized the way back to the city, and he finally made his way back to his mother's house. Exhausted, he sank into her arms and fainted, forgetting even the precious treasures he was carrying in his pockets.

When Aladdin awoke the next day, he was very hungry. But his mother said, 'Alas, my son, I have not even a piece of bread that I could give you.' 'Dear mother,' answered Aladdin, 'give me the lamp I brought with me yesterday. I'll go and sell it. The money will be enough to buy us food for breakfast, lunch, and perhaps even for supper.' The mother fetched the lamp and said, 'Here it is, but it is very dirty. It will be worth a lot more once it has been cleaned.' She took a cloth and started to polish the lamp, but no sooner had she begun to rub it than a gigantic genie emerged from it, asking in a thunderous voice, 'What is your command? Here I am, ready to obey you as your servant and as a servant to those who have the lamp in their hand, both I and all other servants of the lamp.'

When Aladdin and his mother had recovered from their fright, and their excitement about this unexpected good fortune had settled, they decided that they would only ever wish for enough to have a good life without causing envy among their neighbors. As such, they could have lived well until the end of their days. However, one day the sultan's daughter, beautiful Badr al-Budur, visited

the city. As soon as Aladdin set eyes on Badr al-Budur, his heart was enchanted. The princess was the most beautiful woman imaginable, with large, bright and passionate eyes, a gentle gaze, a flawless nose, a small mouth, and lovely pink lips. Aladdin was consumed by thoughts of how to make his greatest wish – to have Badr al-Budur as his wife – come true. He begged his mother to ask the sultan for the princess's hand on Aladdin's behalf. When she replied that it was unlikely she would even be granted access to the palace without a suitable gift, he brushed her doubts aside, because luckily Aladdin remembered the ample treasures he had brought back home with the magic lamp. Treasures that he had since forgotten in his bag. He quickly thought up a plan and arranged his precious stones in a large vase. With this priceless gift, the mother was soon granted an audience in the sultan's palace.

However, while the sultan was impressed by the magnificently shining gems, he had also noticed the mother's humble appearance. To ensure that his future son-in-law would be worthy of the princess's high rank, he demanded proof of Aladdin's wealth. The mother returned home with the order to deliver forty chests filled with gold, precious stones, and the like to the palace. Aladdin was not concerned at all. He fetched the lamp, rubbed it, and asked the genie to do his bidding. The genie complied, and the sultan, speechless with delight about securing such a good marriage for his daughter, was happy to accept Aladdin as Badr al-Budur's future husband.

The wedding was soon celebrated in splendid style. Aladdin did not hesitate to ask the genie in the lamp to build a magnificent palace for him and his bride directly next to the sultan's – and to provide a veritable army of servants at

the couple's disposal. They lacked nothing, and Aladdin even managed to win favor with all of the city's people thanks to the generosity he showed to everyone.

Aladdin couldn't have been more content. But his happiness did not last very long, because the African magician soon heard word that Aladdin had not perished in the cave but was instead living a life of luxury with a beautiful princess by his side and was highly respected by all around him. Again, the magician flew into a rage, and he set out to the city in the Orient where he had failed to make his luck.

Once arrived, fortune was on his side this time, because people in the city spoke about Aladdin being away on an extended hunting trip. The magician sensed an opportunity to regain possession of the precious lamp.

He disguised himself as a lamp merchant, then set up a stall outside the palace gate and began to shout, 'Who will exchange old lamps for new?' Although Badr al-Budur thought that this was a strange offer, it reminded her of the worn old oil lamp on her husband's mantelpiece. As Aladdin had never shared the secret of the lamp with her, she did not hesitate and agreed on an exchange, believing that her husband would be overjoyed about the swap.

The magician took the lamp and immediately began to rub it. Instantly, the genie appeared. 'What is your command?' he asked. 'Here I am, ready to obey you as your servant and as a servant to those who have the lamp in their hand,' his voice thundered. 'I command you,' said the African magician, 'to transport the entire palace with all the people inside to Africa immediately.' No sooner said than done, and in the blink of an

'Who will exchange old lamps for new?'

eye the place next to the sultan's palace was empty. When the sultan awoke the next day, he threw his hands up in disbelief and had his servants call for Aladdin. But Aladdin did not know what to do either upon his return. Once he had searched everywhere in desperation, he realized that it might have been the wicked magician behind the disappearance of the palace. He promised the sultan that he would not rest until he had returned the princess. Luckily, he remembered that he still had at least the ring. He put it on his finger, rubbed it, and in an instant the genie appeared. 'What is your command?' asked the genie. 'Here I am, ready to obey you as your servant and as a servant to those who have the ring on their finger, both I and all other servants of the ring.'

Aladdin answered, 'Genie, save my life for the second time and take me to the place where my wife and my palace are.' No sooner had he spoken these words that the genie transported him to Africa, right under the window of Badr al-Budur's apartment.

When the princess saw her husband, she was barely able to speak she felt so relieved. She whispered to him that she had a secret door unlocked for him so that he would be able to enter the palace unnoticed.

Aladdin told her about the secret of the lamp, and together they made a plan. When the magician sat down for supper with the princess that night, she poured a powder into his glass of wine to punish him for his wickedness. The poison was so powerful that the magician instantly fell into a stupor. Aladdin and the princess searched all of his apartments and finally found the lamp well-hidden underneath his pillow. Aladdin did not lose any time and rubbed the lamp. The genie appeared with his usual greeting. 'Genie,' said Aladdin, 'I have called you to command you by the power of this lamp. Immediately transport this palace back to the Orient, to precisely the same place from which it was taken.'

The genie in the lamp did Aladdin's bidding, and just a moment later the palace was returned to its original site next to the sultan's. The sultan was beside himself with joy and announced ten days of festivities to celebrate the safe return of princess Badr al-Budur and Aladdin. From then on, the princess and Aladdin lived happily and in peace ever after.

A few years later, the sultan died at a very old age. Because he did not have any male heirs, the princess succeeded him to the throne and shared her rule with Aladdin. They governed for many years and had many happy children.

Flavors of the Arabian Nights

Richly aromatic spices, steam rising
from the tagine, and pomegranate seeds sparkling
like the rubies in Aladdin's treasure chamber.
We wouldn't mind a genie in a lamp taking us
to the sultan's palace for a festive meal of delicacies
from the Arabian Nights.

APPETIZER

Tomato salad with pomegranate molasses and sumac

MAIN COURSE

Spiced lamb on polenta

DESSERT

Rosewater-flavored saffron rice pudding

Green pea falafel with lime yogurt

Serves 4

INGREDIENTS

For the falafel:
260 g (9¼ oz) canned chickpeas
250 g (9 oz/1¾ cups) frozen peas
  (defrosted)
2 limes
½ tsp harissa powder
½ tsp ground cumin
½ bunch cilantro
30 g (1 oz) rolled oats
4 tbsp plain (all-purpose) flour
Salt

For the lime yogurt:
1 lime
125 g (4½ oz) Greek yogurt
Salt

Also:
Olive oil for frying
1 pomegranate
½ bunch coriander (cilantro)
1 small red chilli

For the falafel, drain the chickpeas in a strainer and rinse under cold water. Transfer the chickpeas and defrosted peas to a blender. Halve and juice the limes. Add the lime juice, harissa powder, and cumin to the blender and pulse until everything is roughly combined. Transfer the pea mixture to a mixing bowl.

Rinse the coriander, shake dry, and coarsely chop the leaves. Add to the mixture together with the oats and flour and combine everything well. Season the falafel mixture with salt and refrigerate for 30 minutes.

Next, moisten your hands with a little water and shape the mixture into small balls. Press the balls lightly to flatten slightly. Heat a little olive oil in a frying pan and fry the falafel in batches until browned, about 3 minutes per side.

Meanwhile, halve the pomegranate and remove the seeds. Rinse the cilantro, shake dry, and pick off the leaves. Wash, trim, and thinly slice the chilli.

For the lime yogurt, wash the lime under hot water, pat dry, and finely grate the zest. Halve and juice the lime. Combine the lime zest and juice with the yogurt. Season with salt.

Spread the lime yogurt across the center of each plate and arrange the falafel on top. Serve garnished with the chilli, pomegranate seeds, and cilantro.

Tomato salad with pomegranate molasses and sumac

Serves 4

INGREDIENTS

For the salad:
1 tbsp olive oil
8 small, thin slices of bread
1 red onion
1 lemon
Salt
1 kg (2 lb 4 oz) red and
  green tomatoes
½ tsp sumac

For the dressing:
1 lemon
100 g (3½ oz) watermelon
  (without rind)
50 ml (1½ fl oz) olive oil
½ tsp salt
Freshly ground black pepper
50 ml (1½ fl oz) pomegranate
  molasses

Also:
1 handful watercress

For the salad, heat the olive oil in a frying pan. Add the bread slices and toast them until golden on both sides. Keep warm.

For the dressing, halve and juice the lemon. Roughly dice the watermelon. Blend the lemon juice with the watermelon, olive oil, salt, a little pepper, and the pomegranate molasses with a hand-held or regular blender until completely smooth.

Peel the onion and slice it into thin rings. Halve and juice the lemon. Toss the onion rings with the lemon juice and a pinch of salt and set aside for 5 minutes. Meanwhile, wash the tomatoes. Remove the stems and slice thinly.

Rinse the watercress and shake dry. Arrange the sliced tomatoes on plates, drizzle with the dressing, and sprinkle with sumac. Garnish the tomato salad with the onion rings and watercress and serve it with the toasted bread.

Eggplant dip

Serves 4

<u>INGREDIENTS</u>

1 eggplant
2 garlic cloves
30 ml (1 fl oz) olive oil
Sea salt
Freshly ground black pepper
1 lemon

Also:
1 lemon
1 cilantro sprig
Olive oil for drizzling
Bread for serving

Preheat the oven to 210°C (410°F). Wash and trim the eggplant and halve it lengthways. Score the cut surfaces crossways. Peel and thinly slice the garlic.

Transfer the eggplant halves to a baking tray, cut sides up, and brush them with the olive oil. Push the garlic slices inside the scored eggplant flesh. Season the eggplant with sea salt and pepper. Wash the lemon under hot water, pat dry, and finely grate the zest. Sprinkle the lemon zest on top of the eggplant halves. Transfer the tray to the preheated oven (bottom rack) and roast for about 30 minutes.

Cut the lemon into wedges. Rinse the coriander, shake dry, and coarsely chop the leaves. Remove the skin from the roasted eggplant. Finely chop the flesh and transfer it to a serving bowl. Season with a little olive oil and lemon juice. Toss with the cilantro. Serve the eggplant dip with bread.

Middle Eastern salad with figs

Serves 4

INGREDIENTS

400 g (14 oz) couscous
400 ml (14 fl oz) hot vegetable stock
1 tsp cumin seeds
½ tsp coriander seeds
2 tbsp olive oil
1 bunch parsley
3 mint sprigs
1 lemon
2 tomatoes
3 spring onions (scallions)
4 fresh figs
1 tbsp honey
1 small pomegranate

Place the couscous in a bowl. Pour the hot vegetable stock over the couscous, cover the bowl, and leave the couscous to swell for 15 minutes. Once it has absorbed all of the liquid, loosen the couscous with a fork. Finely crush the cumin and coriander seeds using a mortar and pestle. Heat the olive oil in a frying pan and briefly fry the spices until they turn fragrant.

Rinse the parsley and mint and shake dry. Pick off the leaves. Set a few parsley and mint leaves aside for garnish and finely chop the rest. Wash the lemon under hot water and pat dry. Finely peel the zest and cut into very fine matchsticks. Halve and juice the lemon.

Wash the tomatoes, remove the stems, and finely dice. Wash and trim the spring onions and thinly slice them. Toss the tomatoes, spring onion, lemon juice, chopped herbs, cumin, and coriander with the couscous. Set the salad aside for about 15 minutes to allow the flavors to develop.

Wash, trim, and slice the figs. Warm a pan over a low heat. Add the honey and figs to warm through. Halve the pomegranate and carefully remove the seeds. Divide the couscous salad among plates. Serve garnished with the figs, pomegranate seeds, lemon zest, mint, and parsley.

Spicy red dal
with a cilantro dip

Serves 4

INGREDIENTS

For the dal:

1 onion
1 piece fresh ginger
  (about 1 cm/½ inch)
1 tomato
1 red chilli
1 cilantro sprig
2 tbsp sunflower oil
1 heaped tsp cumin seeds
300 g (10½ oz) red lentils
1 tsp salt
½ tsp ground turmeric
2 tsp ground coriander
½ tsp chilli powder
  (or cayenne pepper)

For the cilantro dip:

1 bunch cilantro
1 lemon
125 g (4½ oz) plain yogurt
3 pinches salt

Also:

8 poppadoms
1 small red chilli

For the dal, peel the onion and ginger. Mince the ginger and finely dice the onion. Wash the tomato, remove the stem, and dice finely. Wash, halve, and deseed the chilli. Chop finely. Rinse the cilantro and shake dry. Pick off the leaves and chop finely.

Heat the sunflower oil in a wide saucepan. Add the cumin seeds and fry until fragrant. Add the ginger and onion and cook until lightly browned. Wash the lentils thoroughly and drain. Add the lentils to the saucepan together with about 700 ml (24 fl oz) water, the tomato, chilli, chopped cilantro, salt, turmeric, ground coriander, and chilli powder. Stir through once, bring to a simmer, and continue to cook over a low heat for 15–20 minutes.

For the dip, rinse the cilantro and shake dry. Pick off the leaves and chop them finely. Halve and juice the lemon. Combine the lemon juice, yogurt, cilantro, and salt.

Prepare the poppadoms according to the instructions on the packet. Wash, trim, and thinly slice the chilli. Divide the dal among plates and top with the dip. Garnish with the cilantro and chilli. Serve with the poppadoms.

Chicken and white wine tagine

Serves 4

INGREDIENTS

2 garlic cloves
2 red onions
1 piece fresh ginger
  (about 1 cm/½ inch)
3 tbsp olive oil
4 chicken marylands (leg and
  thigh pieces), separated
Sea salt
Freshly ground black pepper
1 small pinch saffron threads
½ tsp coriander seeds
½ tsp cumin seeds
½ tsp mild paprika
1 cinnamon stick
3 bay leaves
1 tbsp tomato paste
700 ml (24 fl oz) chicken stock
250 ml (9 fl oz/1 cup) white wine

Also:
Tagine dish

Peel the garlic and onion. Quarter the onions and thinly slice the garlic. Peel and mince the ginger.

Preheat the oven to 190°C (375°F). Heat the tagine dish. Add the olive oil, followed by the chicken pieces, and sear on all sides for about 5 minutes. Season with a generous pinch of sea salt and pepper. Stir in the onion and garlic and continue to fry for 4–5 minutes until everything starts to brown.

Add the ginger, saffron, coriander seeds, cumin seeds, paprika, cinnamon stick, and bay leaves. Stir in the tomato paste and fry everything briefly. Add the chicken stock and white wine and bring everything to a boil.

Transfer the tagine to the preheated oven (bottom rack) and cook the chicken until done, about 50 minutes. Divide among plates and serve.

Tip:

This dish goes well with couscous.

Saffron chicken
with barberry rice

Serves 4

INGREDIENTS

1 piece fresh ginger
  (about 2 cm/¾ inch)
3 garlic cloves
1 small red chilli
1 lemon
4 chicken marylands (leg and
  thigh pieces), separated
½ tsp ground cumin
200 g (7 oz) jasmine rice
1 tsp salt
1 heaped tbsp dried barberries,
  cranberries, or currants
1 small pinch saffron threads

Also:
2 flat-leaf parsley sprigs

Peel and mince the ginger and garlic. Wash the chilli, halve it lengthways, and deseed. Chop finely. Wash the lemon under hot water and pat dry. Finely peel the zest and cut into very fine matchsticks. Halve and juice the lemon.

Toss the chicken with the lemon zest and juice in a large mixing bowl. Add the ginger, garlic, chilli, and cumin and combine well. Cover the bowl and leave the meat to marinate in the refrigerator for 3 hours.

Preheat the oven to 170°C (325°F). Combine the jasmine rice with 300 ml (10½ fl oz) water, salt, the dried fruit, and saffron in a large ovenproof frying pan. Arrange the chicken pieces on top. Transfer the pan to the preheated oven (middle rack) and cook the meat until done, about 45 minutes.

Rinse the parsley and shake dry. Pick off the leaves and chop them coarsely. Serve the saffron chicken garnished with the parsley leaves.

Spiced lamb on polenta

Serves 4

INGREDIENTS

For the lamb:
2.5 kg (5 lb 8 oz) leg of lamb
2 lemons
4 garlic cloves
1 tsp cumin seeds
1 tsp coriander seeds
1 small red chilli
1 tsp salt
2 tbsp olive oil
2 star anise
1 cinnamon stick

For the polenta:
250 ml (9 fl oz/1 cup) milk
100 ml (3½ fl oz) chicken stock
30 g (1 oz) butter
1 tsp salt
Freshly ground black pepper
25 g (1 oz) polenta
20 g (¾ oz) parmesan cheese

Also:
½ bunch cilantro

Prepare the lamb by removing any tendons and silver skin from the meat. Wash the lemons under hot water and pat dry. Finely peel the zest from one lemon and cut it into very fine matchsticks. Halve and juice the lemon. Rub the meat with the lemon juice and zest.

Peel and thinly slice the garlic. Crush the cumin and coriander seeds in a mortar and pestle or leave whole if preferred. Wash, trim, and deseed the chilli. Chop finely. Combine the garlic, cumin, coriander, chilli, and salt in a small bowl and massage the spices well into the meat.

Preheat the oven to 160°C (315°F). Heat the olive oil in a large frying pan and sear the meat on all sides. Transfer the meat to a deep roasting dish. Add 1 liter (35 fl oz/4 cups) water, the star anise, and cinnamon stick. Slice the second lemon and arrange the slices on top of the lamb. Place the dish into the preheated oven (bottom rack) and cook the lamb until done, about 2 hours, turning and basting it frequently.

Cook the polenta just before the end of the roasting time. Add the milk, chicken stock, and butter to a saucepan with the salt and pepper. Bring to a boil. Stir in the polenta and simmer over a low heat for about 10 minutes, stirring continuously, until the polenta is soft. Finely grate the parmesan and stir in. If the polenta is too thick, add a little more milk or chicken stock. Season with salt and pepper.

Rinse the cilantro, shake dry, and coarsely chop the leaves. Garnish the cooked lamb with cilantro. Divide the polenta among plates and arrange the lamb on top.

Grilled apricots
with yogurt and honey

Serves 4

INGREDIENTS

1 kg (2 lb 4 oz) ripe apricots
70 g (2½ oz) sugar
500 g (1 lb 2 oz) plain yogurt
2 lemons
50 g (1¾ oz) almonds
3 tbsp honey
1 cinnamon stick
2 star anise

Also:
4 mint sprigs

Wash the apricots and pat dry. Halve the apricots and remove the pits. Divide the apricots into two equal portions. Add one portion to a saucepan together with 100 ml (3½ fl oz) water and 30 g (1 oz) sugar and bring to a boil. Simmer for about 20 minutes over a low heat to reduce the liquid, stirring occasionally. Set aside to cool.

Stir the yogurt until smooth. Layer the yogurt and stewed, cooled apricot halves in glasses or jars.

Take the second apricot portion. Heat a large frying pan. Dip the apricot halves into the remaining sugar. Transfer them to the hot pan and fry until caramelized on both sides. Halve and juice the lemons. Deglaze the apricots in the pan with the lemon juice, then set the pan aside.

Coarsely chop the almonds. Roast the almonds lightly in a frying pan together with the honey, cinnamon, and star anise.

Rinse the mint and shake dry. Arrange the caramelized apricot halves on plates. Top with the honeyed almonds and garnish with sprigs of mint. Serve with the apricot and yogurt in jars or glasses.

Rosewater-flavored
saffron rice pudding

Serves 4

INGREDIENTS

150 g (5 ½ oz/ ¾ cup) basmati rice
100 g (3 ½ oz) sugar
1 pinch salt
1 small pinch saffron threads
20 g (¾ oz) flaked almonds
40 ml (1 ¼ fl oz) rosewater

Also:
1 tbsp flaked almonds
1 tbsp pistachio kernels
1 tbsp dried rose petals

Rinse the basmati rice under cold water in a sieve for a few minutes. Transfer to a saucepan together with 800 ml (28 fl oz) water, the sugar, and salt and bring to a boil. Simmer the rice over a low heat for about 20 minutes or until it starts to take on a porridge-like consistency. Stir frequently. Add a little more water if the rice is still too firm.

Stir in the saffron, almond flakes, and rosewater. Take the rice off the heat and leave to steep for 10 minutes. Divide the rice among four shallow bowls and refrigerate for about 12 hours.

Serve the saffron rice pudding garnished with almond flakes, pistachios, and rose petals.

Power balls

Makes 12 balls

INGREDIENTS

100 g (3 ½ oz) dried figs
100 g (3 ½ oz) dried dates
100 g (3 ½ oz) dried apricots
1 vanilla bean
100 g (3 ½ oz) ground walnuts
50 g (1 ¾ oz) almond butter
1 pinch salt

Also:
100 g (3 ½ oz) coconut flakes

Remove the stalks from the dried figs. Pulse the dried figs, dates, and apricots in a blender to chop finely. Slice the vanilla bean open lengthways and scrape out the seeds.

Transfer the fig mixture to a mixing bowl and knead together with the ground walnuts, almond butter, salt, and vanilla seeds. Next, moisten your hands with a little water and shape evenly sized balls from the mixture.

Place the coconut flakes into a deep bowl and roll the balls in the chips until they are well coated.

Pistachio baklava

Makes 1 square
(about 20 x 20 cm/8 x 8 inches)

INGREDIENTS

For the syrup:
300 g (10½ oz) sugar
300 g (10½ oz) honey
1 lemon

For the baklava:
250 g (9 oz) butter
250 g (9 oz) filo pastry
  (from the refrigerator section)
200 g (7 oz/2 cups) almond meal
150 g (5½ oz) ground walnuts
1 tsp cinnamon

Also:
Oil for the pan (or melted butter)
20 g (¾ oz) pistachios
  for sprinkling

For the syrup, bring the sugar and honey to a boil in a pan with 250 ml (9 fl oz/1 cup) water. Simmer everything over a low heat for about 5 minutes until you have a pale syrup. Halve and juice the lemon. Add the juice to the mixture.

For the baklava, preheat the oven to 190°C (375°F). Brush a 20 x 20 cm (8 x 8 inch) square baking dish with oil. Melt the butter in a saucepan. Cut the filo pastry sheets to the size of the tin. Place one sheet of pastry inside the tin and brush it with melted butter. Combine the almond meal, walnuts, and cinnamon in a separate bowl. Spread a thin layer of the nut mixture on top of the filo pastry sheet. Top with another sheet of pastry and brush with melted butter. Spread again with a little nut mixture and continue until you have used up all of the pastry sheets and filling.

Finish with a sheet of filo pastry and brush with the remaining butter. Use a sharp knife to cut the baklava into 5 cm (2 inch) squares. Transfer the pan to the preheated oven (bottom rack) and bake the baklava for 10 minutes. Drizzle the baklava with the syrup, return it to the oven, and continue to bake for about another 30 minutes. Finely chop the pistachios and sprinkle on top of the baked baklava.

Cinderella

here once lived a rich man, whose wife fell ill, and when she felt that her end was near, she called her only daughter to her bedside and said, 'Dear child, always remain polite and good. I'll look down on you from heaven and will always be with you.' Soon after, she closed her eyes and died. The girl went to visit her mother's grave every day and cried. When winter came, snow covered the grave with a white blanket, and when the spring sun had melted the snow again, the man took another wife.

The new wife brought two daughters into the home with her, who were pretty, but whose hearts were wicked and mean. From then on, hard times began for the poor girl. 'Is this silly goose to sit in the parlour with us?' they said. 'If she wants to eat bread, she'll have to earn it – out with this kitchen maid!' They took her beautiful clothes away, put her into an old, grey smock and gave her wooden shoes. 'Just look at the little princess!' they shouted and laughed, leading the girl into the kitchen. There, she had to do hard work from morning to night, get up before daybreak, carry water, make the fire, cook, and wash. Not only that, but the sisters also made her life even harder wherever they could. They mocked her and scattered peas and lentils into the ashes so that the girl had to sit until late at night and pick them out again. In the evening, when she was tired from her day's chores, she did not have a bed. Instead, she had to sleep in the ashes next to the hearth. And because this made her look dusty and dirty all the time, she was called Cinderella.

'Father, break off for me the first twig that brushes against your hat on your way home.'

One day when the father was going to the fair, he asked his two stepdaughters what he should bring back for them. 'Beautiful dresses,' said the one. 'Pearls and jewels,' said the other. 'And you, Cinderella,' he asked, 'what do you want?' 'Father, break off for me the first twig that brushes against your hat on your way home.' The father bought beautiful dresses, pearls and jewels for the two stepsisters. On the way home, when he was riding through a green thicket, he brushed against a hazel bush, and a twig knocked off his hat. He broke off the twig and took it with him. When he arrived back home, he gave his stepdaughters what they had asked for, and he gave Cinderella the twig from the hazel bush. The girl thanked him, went to her mother's grave, and planted the twig on it, crying so much that her tears fell on it and watered it. Over time, the twig grew into a beautiful tree. Cinderella went to the tree three times a day. Each time she cried, and each time she saw a little bird flutter among its branches. Whenever the girl uttered a wish, the bird threw down to her what she had asked for.

One day, the king announced that there would be a great ball. All of the pretty young girls in the land were invited so that the prince could select a bride for himself. The festivities were to last three days. When the two stepsisters heard that they were also invited, they called Cinderella and told her, 'Comb our hair, polish our shoes, and fasten our buckles. We're going to the ball at the king's castle.' Cinderella obeyed, but cried because she would have dearly loved to go to the ball with them. She asked her stepmother for permission. 'Cinderella,' answered her stepmother, 'you are covered in dust and dirt, and yet want to go to a

ball? You have neither a gown nor shoes and want to dance?' But when Cinderella kept asking, the stepmother said, 'Here, I have scattered a bowl of lentils into the ashes. If you have picked all of them out in two hours' time, you may come with us.' The girl went through the back door into the garden and called out, 'You tame pigeons, you turtledoves, all you little birds beneath the sky, come and help me. The good ones go into the pot, the bad ones go into your crop.'

Two white pigeons immediately came in through the kitchen window, followed by turtledoves, and then all of the little birds beneath the sky fluttered and swarmed inside, settling around the ashes. The pigeons nodded their little heads and began to pick, pick, pick. And all the others started to pick, pick, pick too, sorting all of the good lentils into the bowl. Hardly an hour had passed before they were done and all flew out again. The girl took the bowl to her stepmother, happy in the belief that she would now be allowed to go to the ball with them. But the stepmother said, 'No, Cinderella, you do not have a gown and cannot dance, people will only laugh at

you.' When Cinderella started to cry, the stepmother said, 'If you pick two bowls of lentils from the ashes in one hour, you may come,' thinking by herself that the girl would never be able to do that. After the stepmother had scattered two bowls of lentils into the ashes, the girl went through the back door into the garden and called out, 'You tame pigeons, you turtledoves, all you little birds beneath the sky, come and help me. The good ones go into the pot, the bad ones go into your crop.'

Two white pigeons immediately came in through the kitchen window, followed by turtledoves, and then all of the little birds beneath the sky fluttered and swarmed inside, settling around the ashes. And the pigeons nodded their little heads and began to pick, pick, pick. And all the others started to pick, pick, pick too, sorting all of the good lentils into the bowls. Hardly half an hour had passed before they were done and all flew out again. The girl took the bowls to her stepmother, happy in the belief that she would now be allowed to go to the ball with them. But the stepmother said, 'It's no use. You cannot come because you do not have a gown and cannot dance. We would be ashamed of you.' With that, she turned her back on poor Cinderella and hurried away with her two proud daughters.

Now that Cinderella was alone at home, she went to her mother's grave underneath the hazel tree and called, 'Shake and quiver, little tree, throw gold and silver down to me.'

And the bird threw a silver and golden gown down to her and slippers embroidered in silk and silver. Cinderella quickly put on the gown and ran to the ball. Her stepsisters and stepmother did not recognize her and thought that she must be a princess from a foreign land, so beautiful did the girl look in her golden gown. They did not even think about Cinderella, believing her to still be sitting at home in the dirt, picking out lentils from the ashes. The prince approached Cinderella, took her by the hand, and danced with her. Furthermore, he refused to dance with anyone else and did not let go of her hand. Every

time another man asked Cinderella for a dance, the prince said, 'She dances with me.'

They danced until the evening, and when Cinderella said that she wanted to go home, the prince said, 'I'll go with you and accompany you,' because he wanted to see where this beautiful girl lived. But Cinderella eluded him and jumped into the pigeon coop to hide. The prince waited until her father came and told him that the strange girl had jumped into the coop. The old man wondered whether it had been Cinderella. He asked for an axe and a pick to be brought to him to split the pigeon coop but did not find anyone inside. And when they got home, there was Cinderella lying in the ashes in her dirty clothes, and a dim oil lamp was burning in the fireplace. Cinderella had quickly jumped out from the back of the pigeon coop and had run to the hazel tree. There, she had taken off her beautiful gown and slippers and laid them on her mother's grave. The bird had taken them away again, while Cinderella put

on her grey smock and sat down in the ashes next to the kitchen hearth.

The next day, when the ball was to begin anew and the parents and stepsisters had again left, Cinderella went back to the hazel tree and said, 'Shake and quiver, little tree, throw gold and silver down to me.'

This time, the bird threw down an even more splendid gown than on the day before. When Cinderella appeared at the ball in the gown, she astounded everyone with her beauty. The prince was already waiting for her. He immediately took Cinderella by the hand and danced with her alone. Whenever another man asked her for a dance, he said, 'She dances with me.' When Cinderella again wanted to go home that night, the prince followed her to see into which house she would go. But the girl ran away from him into the garden behind the house. There stood a beautiful tall tree carrying the most magnificent pears. She climbed into its branches as nimbly as a squirrel, and the prince did not know where she had gone. He waited until her father came and told him, 'The strange girl has eluded me, and I believe that she has climbed into your pear tree.' The father again asked himself whether it could have been Cinderella. He had an axe brought to him and felled the tree, but there was no one in it. When they went into the kitchen, there was Cinderella in her usual place, because she had jumped down on the other side of the tree. She had taken her beautiful gown back to the bird on the hazel tree and had put on her grey smock again.

On the third day, as soon as the parents and sisters had left, Cinderella once again went to her mother's grave and asked the tree. 'Shake and quiver, little tree, throw gold and silver down to me.' This time, the bird threw down a gown that was even more dazzling and magnificent than the others, and the slippers were of pure gold. When Cinderella arrived at the ball in her gown, the other guests were so astonished that they did not know what to say. The prince danced with her alone, and every time another man asked her for a dance, he said, 'She dances with me.'

When evening came, Cinderella had to leave, and the prince wanted to accompany her, but she eluded him so quickly that he could not follow her. But the clever prince had made a plan and had the entire stairway covered with tar. When Cinderella ran down the stairs, her left slipper got stuck in the pitch. The prince picked it up. It was a small, dainty slipper made entirely of gold. The next morning, he took the slipper to the father and said, 'None other shall be my wife than the one whose foot fits this golden shoe.' The two sisters were very happy to hear this, because they had pretty feet. The oldest took the slipper to her chamber to try it on with her mother standing next to her. But she could not get her big toe into the slipper, which was too small for her. So her mother gave her a knife and said, 'Cut off your toe. Once you are queen, you will no longer have to go on foot.' The girl cut off her toe, forced the foot inside the slipper, and swallowed her pain. Then she went out to meet the prince again. He took her on his horse as his bride and rode away with her. But they had to ride past the grave and there, on the hazel tree, sat the two pigeons, calling, 'Rook di goo, rook di goo! There's blood in the shoe. The shoe is too tight, this bride is not right!'

> 'Shake and quiver, little tree, throw gold and silver down to me.'

145

When the prince heard this, he looked at the girl's foot and saw blood running from it. He turned his horse around and took the false bride home again, saying that this was not the right one and the other sister should put on the shoe. The second sister went into her chamber. She got her toes into the slipper just fine, but her heel was too large. So her mother gave her a knife and said, 'Cut off a piece of your heel. Once you are queen, you will no longer have to go on foot.' The girl cut off a piece of her heel, forced the foot inside the slipper, and swallowed her pain. Then she went out to meet the prince again. He took her on his horse as his bride and rode away with her. But when they passed the hazel tree, there sat the two pigeons, calling, 'Rook di goo, rook di goo! There's blood in the shoe. The shoe is too tight, this bride is not right!'

The prince looked down at the girl's foot and saw that there was blood running from it and that it had stained her white stockings bright red. He turned his horse around and took the false bride home again. 'This is not the right bride either,' he said. 'Don't you have another daughter?' 'No,' said the father, 'there is only a pitiful little Cinderella here from my first wife, but she cannot possibly be the bride.' The prince asked to see her, but the mother answered, 'Oh, no, she is much too dirty and cannot be seen.' But the prince insisted, and they had to call for Cinderella. Cinderella washed her hands and face and then bowed before the prince, who passed her the golden slipper. Cinderella sat down on a stool, pulled her foot out of her heavy wooden shoe, and put it into the slipper. It fitted her perfectly. And when she stood up and looked the prince into his eyes, he instantly recognized the beautiful girl who had danced with him. He cried, 'This is my true bride!' The stepmother and two sisters were horrified and turned pale with anger, but he took Cinderella on his horse and rode away with her. When they passed the hazel tree, the two pigeons called, 'Rook di goo, rook di goo! No blood in the shoe. The shoe is not too tight, this bride is right!' And after they had sung this, the two pigeons flew down and sat on Cinderella's shoulders, one on the right, one on the left, and stayed there.

On the day of Cinderella's and the prince's wedding, the wicked sisters came and wanted to gain favor with Cinderella and share her good fortune. As the bride and groom walked to the church, the older sister walked on their right and the younger on their left side. Then came the pigeons and pecked out one eye from each of them. When the couple stepped outside the church again after the ceremony, the older sister walked on their left and the younger on their right side. Then came the pigeons and pecked out the other eye from each of them. Thus they were punished for their wickedness and falsehood with blindness for the rest of their lives.

'Rook di goo, rook di goo! No blood in the shoe. The shoe is not too tight, this bride is right!'

Princely indulgence

The good ones go into the pot, the bad ones go into your crop . . . Well, we'll happily leave humble legumes to the wicked stepmother. We'd rather dance at the king's ball together with Cinderella and indulge in an opulent feast of luxurious delicacies for which the prince might even be prepared to forget about the golden slipper.

APPETIZER

Meatball soup

MAIN COURSE

Pork fillets with rosemary, lime, and squash purée

DESSERT

Petits Fours

Canapés three ways

Serves 4

INGREDIENTS

For the curry cappuccino:
1 garlic clove
2 French shallots
1 small tart apple
2 button mushrooms
2 tbsp butter
¼ tsp sugar
2 tbsp curry powder
300 ml (10½ fl oz) chicken stock
  (or beef stock)
100 ml (3½ fl oz) heavy cream
10 kitchen-ready prawns (shrimp)
1 tbsp olive oil

For the puff pastry:
1–2 sheets puff pastry
  (about 275 g/9¾ oz)
100 g (3½ oz) button mushrooms
1 tsp raspberry or sherry vinegar
2 tbsp olive oil
5 cherry tomatoes

For the beef tartare:
200 g (7 oz) beef rump steak
2 tbsp grapeseed oil
2½ tbsp soy sauce, divided
1 tbsp yuzu juice or lime juice
200 g (7 oz) kabocha squash
1 tsp mirin (or sugar)
1 tbsp lemon juice

Also:
Salt, sea salt
Freshly ground black pepper
Parsley and thyme for garnish

For the curry cappuccino, peel and mince the garlic and shallots. Peel, core, and finely dice the apple. Trim, clean, and finely dice the button mushrooms. Heat the butter in a small saucepan until foamy. Add the prepared shallots, apple, button mushrooms, and garlic and sweat over a low heat for a few minutes. Stir in the sugar and curry powder. Pour in the chicken stock and simmer gently for about 8 minutes. Add the cream and continue to simmer for a little longer. Finely blend the soup with a hand-held blender and pass it through a sieve if you like. Season with salt and pepper.

Season the prawns with salt and pepper. Heat the olive oil in a frying pan, toss in the prawns, and fry for about 1 minute per side. Divide the curry cappuccino among cups or small glasses. Top with the prawns and garnish with a little parsley to serve.

For the puff pastry, preheat the oven to 210°C (410°F). Line a baking tray with baking paper. Cut the puff pastry into 3 cm (1¼ inch) squares. Transfer the pastry squares to the baking tray and bake them in the preheated oven (middle rack) until golden, about 15 minutes. Set aside to cool.

Meanwhile clean, trim, and thinly slice the button mushrooms. Toss with the vinegar, olive oil, and a little salt and pepper. Set the mushrooms aside for about 10 minutes to marinate. Wash and slice the cherry tomatoes. Top the pastry squares with the cherry tomato and mushroom slices. Garnish with parsley and sprinkle with sea salt to serve.

For the beef tartare, mince the beef rump steak and combine with the grapeseed oil, 1½ tbsp soy sauce, yuzu or lime juice, and a little pepper. Set the tartare aside for 10 minutes to marinate, then shape it into small balls. Wash and trim the squash and cut it into paper-thin slices. Toss with the mirin, lemon juice, and remaining soy sauce. Set aside for 10 minutes. Place the tartare balls on individual spoons and garnish with the squash slices and thyme leaves to serve.

Beluga lentil salad

Serves 4

INGREDIENTS

For the salad:
300 g (10½ oz) beluga
   (black) lentils
2 ripe mangoes
4 French shallots
2 spring onions (scallions)
1 tbsp olive oil
1 tbsp pine nuts
Salt

For the marinade:
½ small red chilli
1 garlic clove
3 tbsp balsamic vinegar
1 tbsp lemon juice
2 tbsp dark sesame oil
2 tbsp soy sauce
2 tbsp mirin (or sugar)
100 ml (3½ fl oz) apple juice
4 tbsp Styrian pumpkin seed oil
   (or other pumpkin seed oil,
   available at health food stores)

Also:
2 cilantro sprigs

For the salad, rinse the beluga lentils under cold water in a sieve. Next, bring the lentils to a boil in a saucepan with plenty of water. Cook until soft (about 30 minutes) over a low heat. Drain and set aside.

Meanwhile, peel and thinly slice the mangoes. Peel and finely dice the shallots. Wash and trim the spring onions, then thinly slice them diagonally. Heat the olive oil in a frying pan. Add the pine nuts and toast until golden brown. Season with salt and set aside to cool.

For the marinade, wash, trim, and deseed the chilli. Chop finely. Peel and mince the garlic. Whisk both with the vinegar, lemon juice, sesame oil, soy sauce, mirin, apple juice, and pumpkin seed oil in a bowl.

Rinse the cilantro, shake dry, and pick off the leaves. Combine the diced shallots with the marinade. Toss the lentils in the marinade and divide them among plates. Garnish with the spring onion, toasted pine nuts, sliced mango, and cilantro, and serve.

Mini blini with beetroot, horseradish, and salmon

Serves 4

INGREDIENTS

For the blini:
110 g (3¾ oz/¾ cup) plain
  (all-purpose) flour
110 g (3¾ oz/¾ cup) spelt flour
2 eggs
250 ml (9 fl oz/1 cup) buttermilk
20 g (¾ oz) fresh yeast
Salt
2 tbsp sunflower oil

For the beetroot cream:
100 g (3½ oz) cooked beetroot
  (beets)
50 g (1¾ oz) quark or cream cheese
2 tbsp mayonnaise
½ tsp salt
Freshly ground black pepper
1 tsp grated horseradish

Also:
125 g (4½ oz) smoked salmon
1 small jar salmon caviar
  (to taste)
1 handful pea sprouts
Grated fresh horseradish
  for garnish

For the blini, sift the two types of flour into a mixing bowl. Separate the eggs. Gently warm the buttermilk until it is lukewarm. Crumble the yeast and stir it into the warm buttermilk. Add the buttermilk and yeast mixture to the flour. Stir in the egg yolks. Cover the bowl and leave the batter to rise for about 30 minutes. Add the salt to the egg whites and beat until stiff. Gently fold the egg whites into the batter.

Heat a little sunflower oil in a frying pan. Use a spoon to transfer pikelet-sized (about 7.5 cm/3 inches diameter) amounts of batter to the pan. Cook the blini until golden, about 2 minutes per side.

For the beetroot cream, coarsely chop the beetroot and blend finely with a hand-held or benchtop blender. Add the cream cheese, mayonnaise, salt, a little pepper, and the horseradish and continue to blend to make a smooth cream. Pass the mixture through a fine sieve if you prefer.

Top the blini with the smoked salmon and caviar to taste. Garnish with the pea sprouts and a little grated horseradish. Serve with the beetroot cream.

Meatball soup

Serves 4

INGREDIENTS

For the beef stock:

1 large onion
250 g (9 oz) soup vegetables
  (e.g. carrots, celeriac, parsley root/
  Hamburg parsley, leek, and parsley)
1 kg (2 lb 4 oz) beef (e.g. shoulder
  blade, beef shank, or fillet)
2 juniper berries
2 bay leaves
5 black peppercorns
Salt
Freshly grated nutmeg

For the bone marrow dumplings:

60 g (2¼ oz) white bread
  (crust removed)
100 g (3½ oz) bone marrow
  (from a butcher)
1 egg
50 g (1¾ oz/⅓ cup) plain
  (all-purpose) flour
60 g (2¼ oz) breadcrumbs
½ tsp salt
Freshly ground black pepper
1 parsley sprig

For the pancakes:

150 ml (5 fl oz) milk
50 g (1¾ oz/⅓ cup) plain
  (all-purpose) flour
½ tsp salt
1 egg
2 tbsp sunflower oil

Also:

1 bunch chives

For the beef stock, halve the onion (unpeeled). Line a frying pan with foil and turn on the heat. Place the onion halves on the hot foil, cut side down, and cook until almost blackened. Wash, trim, and coarsely chop the soup vegetables. Bring about 4 liters (140 fl oz/16 cups) water to the boil in a large pot, then add the beef. Simmer the meat for about 1 hour.

Add the soup vegetables, onion halves, juniper berries, bay leaves, and pepper and continue to simmer everything for another 2–3 hours. Add more water if necessary. The beef should always be covered with liquid. Skim any foam off the surface throughout. Strain the stock and season with salt and nutmeg; remove the bay leaves. Cut the beef and vegetables into small pieces.

For the bone marrow dumplings, finely dice the white bread and soak the pieces briefly in water. Next, squeeze out any excess water and chop the bread finely. Pass the bone marrow through a sieve. Whisk the egg, then add the marrow and beat the mixture until foamy. Stir in the soaked bread, flour, and breadcrumbs. Season the dumpling mixture with salt and pepper.

Rinse the parsley and shake dry. Finely chop the leaves, then add them to the mixture. Shape the mixture into small dumplings. Bring a large pot of salted water to a boil. Add the dumplings, reduce the heat to low, and simmer for about 6 minutes – do not allow the liquid to boil!

For the pancakes, combine the milk and flour, then whisk in the salt and egg. Heat a non-stick frying pan (24 cm/9½ inches in diameter) with a little oil. Ladle in just enough of the batter to cover the pan thinly. Hold the pan at a slight angle and rotate to spread the batter evenly. Turn the pancakes once bubbles appear on the surface and the bottom is golden brown. Continue with the remaining batter. Set the pancakes aside to cool, then roll them up and slice them thinly.

Rinse the chives, shake them dry, then slice thinly. Serve the soup with the pancake strips, dumplings, vegetables, beef, and chives.

Savory tartlets
with nut pesto

Makes 4

INGREDIENTS

For the tartlets:
500 g (1 lb 2 oz) onions
4 thyme sprigs
2 tbsp olive oil
1 bay leaf
Salt
Freshly ground black pepper
125 g (4½ oz) filo pastry
  (from the refrigerator section)
20 g (¾ oz) black olives
1 rosemary sprig
40 g (1½ oz) feta (sheep's cheese)
30 g (1 oz) frozen English spinach
  (defrosted)
Pink peppercorns
Sea salt

For the nut pesto:
100 g (3½ oz) walnuts
1 lemon
30 g (1 oz) parmesan cheese
2 parsley sprigs
100 ml (3½ fl oz) olive oil
Salt
Freshly ground black pepper

Also:
Butter for the pans

For the tartlets, peel and thinly slice the onions. Rinse and shake the thyme dry. Heat the olive oil in a large frying pan over a low heat. Add the sliced onion, bay leaf, 3 thyme sprigs, and a little salt and pepper. Sweat for about 20 minutes, stirring frequently. Leave to cool.

Preheat the oven to 180°C (350°F). Butter four 9 cm diameter tartlet pans, and line them with the pastry. Tuck any overhanging pastry ends in. Divide the onion among the pans. Fill the tartlet shells with the black olives, rosemary, diced or crumbled feta, remaining thyme, and spinach. Sprinkle with the pink peppercorns and sea salt. Transfer the pans to the preheated oven (middle rack) and bake them until golden brown, about 20 minutes.

Meanwhile, dry-roast the walnuts for the pesto over a low heat, then set them aside to cool. Wash the lemon under hot water, pat dry, and finely grate the zest. Finely dice the parmesan. Rinse the parsley, shake dry, and pick off the leaves. Blend the nuts, olive oil, parmesan, parsley leaves, and lemon zest to make a smooth pesto, using either a hand-held or a regular blender. Season with salt and pepper. Serve the tartlets with the nut pesto.

Pork fillets
with rosemary, lime,
and squash purée

Serves 4

INGREDIENTS

For the squash purée:
1 onion
2 garlic cloves
500 g (1 lb 2 oz) kabocha squash
2 tbsp sunflower oil
150 ml (5 fl oz) vegetable stock
125 g (4½ oz) crème fraîche
Salt
Freshly ground black pepper
1 tbsp Styrian pumpkin seed oil
  (or other pumpkin seed oil,
  available at health food stores)

For the pork fillet:
2 garlic cloves
1 lime
2 tbsp sundried tomatoes in oil
1 rosemary sprig
2 pork fillets (400 g/14 oz each)
Salt
Freshly ground black pepper
3 tbsp olive oil

For the purée, peel the onion and garlic. Mince the garlic and finely dice the onion. Wash, trim, and halve the squash. Remove the seeds and cut the flesh into small pieces. Heat the sunflower oil in a saucepan. Add the garlic and onion and sweat briefly. Add the squash and again sweat briefly.

Stir in the stock and simmer everything over a low heat for about 20 minutes. Add the crème fraîche and blend the mixture finely using a hand-held blender. Season the purée with salt and pepper.

For the pork fillet, preheat the oven to 180°C (350°F). Peel and thinly slice the garlic. Wash the lime under hot water, pat dry, and finely grate the zest. Drain and finely chop the sundried tomatoes. Rinse the rosemary and shake dry. Pick off and chop the leaves.

Combine the rosemary, garlic, sundried tomatoes, and lime zest. Remove any tendons and fat from the pork fillets and season the meat with salt and pepper. Heat the olive oil in an ovenproof frying pan and sear the fillets on both sides. Spread the garlic and tomato mixture evenly over the meat.

Transfer the pan to the preheated oven (middle rack) and cook the fillets until done, about 10 minutes. Turn off the oven and keep the oven door ajar. Leave the meat to rest for 5 minutes at about 50°C (120°F). Halve the fillets and divide the meat among plates. Drizzle the purée with the pumpkin seed oil and serve with the pork fillets.

Duck breast
with butternut squash
and mushrooms

Serves 4

INGREDIENTS

For the meat:
2 duck breast fillets
Salt
2 garlic cloves
2 thyme sprigs

For the sides:
300 g (10½ oz) butternut squash
2 king oyster or king brown
  mushrooms
1 thyme sprig
1 tbsp sunflower oil

For the gravy:
2 tbsp honey
2 tbsp soy sauce
200 ml (7 fl oz) chicken stock

For the meat, gently score the duck breast fillets crossways on the skin side without slicing into the meat. Season the fillets with salt. Peel and mince the garlic. Rinse and shake the thyme dry.

For the sides, peel, trim, and finely dice the butternut squash. Clean and trim the mushrooms and slice them lengthways. Rinse and shake dry the thyme sprig.

Preheat the oven to 80°C (175°F). Transfer the duck breast fillets to an unheated frying pan, skin side down. Heat the pan over a low heat and slowly brown the meat for about 8 minutes. Add the garlic and thyme. Baste the fillets with the juices collected in the pan, turn them, and continue to fry for another 2 minutes on the other side. Remove the fillets from the pan and transfer them to the preheated oven (middle rack) to rest for 6 minutes on a baking tray. The duck breast should be medium rare.

Meanwhile, to prepare the gravy, stir the honey and soy sauce into the meat juices reserved in the pan. Simmer briefly to reduce. Stir in the chicken stock and reduce again. Heat the sunflower oil in a separate frying pan, add the squash, mushrooms, and thyme and sear for a few minutes. Stir in the gravy and continue to simmer for about 3 minutes.

Divide the duck breast fillets into portions, arrange them on plates with the squash and mushrooms, and serve.

Tip:

This dish goes well with polenta or a baguette on the side.

Rice pudding soufflé with pears

**Makes 2 ramekins
(10 cm/4 inches diameter each)**

INGREDIENTS

For the rice pudding soufflé:
20 g (¾ oz) basmati rice
570 ml (20 fl oz) milk
30 g (1 oz) butter
30 g (1 oz) plain (all-purpose) flour
3 eggs
80 g (2¾ oz) sugar

For the pears:
2 pears
250 ml (9 fl oz/1 cup) white wine
1 star anise
1 cinnamon stick
50 g (1¾ oz) sugar

Also:
Butter and flour for the ramekins
Icing (confectioners') sugar
  for dusting

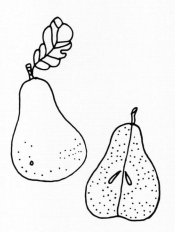

For the rice pudding soufflé, butter the ramekins and dust them with flour. Bring the basmati rice and 400 ml (14 fl oz) milk to a boil in a saucepan. Simmer until soft over a low heat, about 20 minutes. Set aside to cool, then refrigerate for a few hours. You'll need 150 g (5½ oz) rice pudding.

Melt the butter in a saucepan. Stir in the flour, then add 170 ml (5½ fl oz/⅔ cup) milk. Bring the mixture to a boil, stirring continuously, and simmer until it thickens into a smooth béchamel sauce. Set aside to cool, then fold into the rice pudding.

Place a roasting dish filled with about 2 cm (¾ inches) water inside the oven (middle rack) and preheat the oven to 200°C (400°F). Separate the eggs. Combine the egg yolks with the rice pudding mixture. Whisk the egg whites until semi-stiff, then gradually add in the sugar. Continue to whisk until you have stiff peaks. Fold the egg whites into the rice pudding mixture. Divide the mixture among the ramekins. Transfer the ramekins to the baking dish with the hot water. Bake the rice pudding soufflés in the preheated oven until golden brown on top, about 25 minutes.

Meanwhile, peel and quarter the pears lengthways, removing the cores. Combine the white wine, star anise, cinnamon stick, and sugar in a saucepan and bring to a boil. Add the quartered pears and simmer for about 10 minutes.

Dust the rice pudding soufflés with icing sugar and serve with the poached pears.

Swiss roll with meringue topping

Mini almond friands

Scrumptious nut biscuits with strawberries

Petits Fours

Swiss roll with meringue topping

Makes 2 Swiss rolls

INGREDIENTS

For the sponge mix:
5 eggs
1 lemon
50 g (1¾ oz) icing
   (confectioners') sugar
1 pinch salt
½ tsp vanilla extract
70 g (2½ oz) sugar
120 g (4¼ oz) plain
   (all-purpose) flour

For the meringue topping:
100 g (3½ oz) egg whites
200 g (7 oz) caster (superfine)
   sugar

Also:
100 g (3½ oz) apricot jam

Separate the eggs for the sponge mix. Wash the lemon under hot water, pat dry, and finely grate the zest. Whisk the egg yolks, icing sugar, salt, vanilla, and lemon zest until thick and creamy.

Beat the egg whites until semi-stiff. Gradually add the sugar and continue to beat everything until stiff peaks form. Fold the egg whites into the egg yolk mixture. Sift the flour and carefully fold it into the mixture.

Preheat the oven to 220°C (425°F). Line a baking tray with baking paper. Spread the sponge mix evenly across the baking paper and bake it in the preheated oven (middle rack) until golden, about 8 minutes. Leave the oven on.

Set the sponge aside to cool for 2 minutes. Flip the sponge onto another sheet of baking paper and peel off the first sheet of paper. Spread the apricot jam evenly across the sponge. Halve the sponge lengthways and roll up each half from the long side.

For the meringue topping, place a metal bowl over a double boiler over a low heat. Add the egg whites and sugar and, using hand-held electric beaters, whisk for about 5 minutes. Remove the bowl from the double boiler and continue to whisk until cool for at least another 5 minutes. Transfer the meringue mixture to a piping bag with a star-shaped nozzle.

Cut the Swiss rolls into 2–3 cm (¾–1¼ inch) slices. Place half the slices onto a baking tray, cut side up, and pipe some of the meringue mixture on top. Return to the preheated oven (middle rack) until the meringue starts to take on color, for about 3 minutes. Alternatively, caramelize the meringue toppings with a blow torch. Dust the remaining slices with icing sugar to serve.

Petits Fours

Mini almond friands

Makes 20

INGREDIENTS

120 g (4¼ oz/1 cup) icing
  (confectioners') sugar
90 g (3¼ oz) almond meal
25 g (1 oz) plain (all-purpose) flour
170 g (6 oz) butter
2 eggs

Also:
Oil for the molds
200 g (7 oz) raspberries
Icing (confectioners') sugar
  for dusting

Combine the icing sugar, almond meal, and flour in a bowl. Heat the butter in a small saucepan until it takes on a golden-brown color. Stir the eggs and the melted butter into the flour mixture and combine everything well.

Preheat the oven to 200°C (400°F). Brush 20 small silicone molds (2–3 cm/¾–1¼ inches in diameter) with oil and place them on a baking tray. Fill them with the batter and bake them in the preheated oven (middle rack) for 9–11 minutes. Remove the friands from the oven and set them aside to cool before unmolding them.

Garnish the friands with raspberries and serve them dusted with icing sugar.

Petits Fours

Scrumptious nut biscuits with strawberries

Makes about 30

INGREDIENTS

100 g (3½ oz) butter, softened
40 g (1½ oz/⅓ cup) icing
  (confectioners') sugar
1 pinch salt
¼ tsp vanilla extract
1 egg yolk
200 g (7 oz/1⅓ cups) plain
  (all-purpose) flour
50 g (1¾ oz/½ cup) almond meal

Also:
200 ml (7 fl oz) heavy cream
200 g (7 oz) strawberries

Combine the butter, icing sugar, salt, and vanilla in a mixing bowl and whisk until foamy. Stir in the egg yolk. Add the flour and almond meal and knead everything to make a smooth dough. Divide the dough into two equal portions and roll these into logs about 2 cm (¾ inch) thick. Wrap the logs in plastic wrap and refrigerate them for 2 hours.

Preheat the oven to 180°C (350°F). Line a baking tray with baking paper. Cut the dough logs into 1 cm (½ inch) slices and transfer the slices onto the baking tray. Bake the biscuits in the preheated oven (middle rack) until golden, about 15 minutes. Set aside to cool.

Whip the cream until stiff and transfer it to a piping bag. Wash, pat dry, and halve the strawberries. Pipe a little cream on top of each biscuit, garnish with a halved strawberry, and serve.

Hazelnut and chocolate parfait

Serves 4

INGREDIENTS

For the parfait:
1 vanilla bean
200 ml (7 fl oz) milk
5 egg yolks
100 g (3½ oz) sugar
500 ml (17 fl oz/2 cups)
  heavy cream
350 g (12 oz) dark chocolate

For the caramelized hazelnuts:
20 g (¾ oz) sugar
100 g (3½ oz) hazelnuts

For the pears:
1 lemon
2 pears
30 g (1 oz) sugar

For the parfait, slice the vanilla bean open lengthways and scrape out the seeds. Bring the milk, vanilla seeds, and bean to a boil in a saucepan. Combine the egg yolks and the sugar in a mixing bowl. Quickly whisk the hot vanilla milk into the egg yolk mixture. Return the mixture to the saucepan and whisk until creamy over a low heat. Do not allow the mixture to boil or heat to more than 83°C (181°F).

Whip the cream until stiff. Finely chop the chocolate and transfer it to a mixing bowl. Strain the egg yolk and milk mixture into the bowl through a fine sieve and stir to melt the chocolate. Set aside to cool, then fold in the whipped cream. Pour the parfait mixture about 2 cm (¾ inch) deep into a freezer-safe container. Cover and freeze for about 12 hours.

For the caramelized hazelnuts, combine the sugar and 50 ml (1½ fl oz) water in a saucepan and bring to a boil. Add the hazelnuts and stir continuously until the hazelnuts are coated in crystalized sugar and there is no more liquid left in the saucepan. Spread the nuts onto a baking tray to cool, then chop them coarsely.

For the pears, halve and juice the lemon. Wash and peel the pears and slice them lengthways about 1 cm (½ inch) thick. Heat the sugar in a large frying pan or wide saucepan and allow it to caramelize slowly. Only stir when the sugar takes on too much color. Keep shaking the pan. Add the sliced pears and brown on both sides. Deglaze with the lemon juice and take the pan off the heat. Leave the pears to cool in the syrup.

Slice the parfait, divide it among plates, and leave it to stand briefly in order to soften. Garnish with the pears and a little pear syrup and top with the caramelized hazelnuts.

The Snow
Queen

ne day, the devil was in a peculiar mood, and so he decided to create a mirror that had the power to shrink all that was good and beautiful in its reflection into mere nothingness. Everything worthless and cruel, in contrast, was magnified. In this mirror, the most beautiful landscape looked like overcooked spinach, and the very best people became repugnant. The devil flew around with the mirror until there was finally not a land nor person on earth that had not been distorted. But suddenly the mirror shook so terribly under the devil's grip that it slipped out of his hands and fell down to the earth, where it broke into a hundred million pieces.

However, this caused even bigger misfortunes than before. Some of the splinters were now only as small as a grain of sand and were blown around throughout the world. When they were blown into anyone's eyes, they remained stuck, and then the unfortunate people saw everything in a bad light. Some people even had splinters embedded in their hearts. When this happened, their hearts froze into a clump of ice.

In a large town there once lived a boy and a girl named Kai and Gerda. Their parents lived next door to each other in two attics, and in summer the children played beneath the beautiful rose bushes planted between their homes. In winter, however, the windows often frosted over completely. The children would then heat coins on the stove and press them against the glass to make perfect little peepholes, behind which their eyes shone. When thick snow fell outside the window, the grandmother said, 'That's white bees swarming.' 'Do they have a queen bee, too?' asked the little boy. 'Yes, they do,' answered the grandmother. 'Sometimes, around midnight, she buzzes through the town's streets and looks through the windows. They then freeze over in a peculiar fashion and look like magnificent, glittering flowers.'

In the evening, Kai climbed on a chair by the window and looked out through his peephole. As the snow was falling outside, the biggest snowflake of all came to a rest on the edge of a flower box. It grew and grew and turned into the image of a woman, dressed in the finest of clothes made of millions of star-shaped flakes. She was beautiful, but she was made entirely of blinding, shining ice. She nodded to Kai and waved her hand. The little boy became frightened and jumped off the chair.

Finally, spring returned. The sun shone, green grass sprouted, and the children met again to play outside. Those were splendid days! One day, Kai and Gerda were looking at a picture book together, when Kai cried, 'Ouch! Something hurt my heart and then blew into my eye!' It was one of the glass splinters from the evil, magic mirror. A fragment had pierced poor Kai's little heart, which would now soon turn to ice, and while it no longer hurt, the splinter still sat there.

'Why are you crying?' he asked. 'It makes you look ugly! Ugh!' he called suddenly. 'The rose over there is worm-eaten! And that one's crooked!' He then kicked the flower box with his foot and broke off both of the roses. 'Kai, what are you doing?' asked Gerda fearfully. When he saw that he had upset her, he broke off another rose.

Months went by, and one winter's day, Kai came down with his sled on his back and called for Gerda. 'I'm allowed to play in the big square, where the other boys are,' he said, and away he ran.

As he was playing, a large white sleigh drove into the square. On it sat a driver, wrapped in a white fur coat and wearing a white cap. The sleigh drove around the square, and Kai tied his sled to its back to hitch a ride. The sleigh picked up speed and went straight down the next street. The driver turned around and nodded to Kai in a friendly fashion; it was as if they knew each other. Every time Kai wanted to untie his sled, the driver nodded to him again and Kai stayed where he was, until they finally drove out of the town's gates. It started to snow so heavily that the little boy could hardly see his hand in front of his eyes. He let go of the rope holding his sled to unfasten himself from the sleigh, but to no avail. He called out loudly, but there was no one to hear him.

The snowflakes became larger and larger, and suddenly they parted. The large sleigh stopped, and as the driver rose it turned out that the fur coat and cap were entirely made of snow. The driver was a lady, tall and slender and blindingly white – it was the Snow Queen herself.

'You aren't cold, are you?' she asked. 'Quick, crawl under my coat.' And she sat down next to him and wrapped him in her fur coat. Then the Snow Queen kissed little Kai on the forehead. Oh, that kiss felt colder than ice, and its coldness went right to Kai's heart. He thought that he was about to die, but only for a moment, and then he felt nothing more. She kissed him again, and he forgot Gerda, his grandmother, and every-body at home.

Kai looked at the Snow Queen. He could not imagine a cleverer or more beautiful face. She no longer seemed to be made of ice to him, as she had seemed when he first saw her outside of his window, when she had waved at him. In his eyes, she was perfect. The Snow Queen flew with him over forests and lakes, over many lands and seas.

But how did little Gerda fare when Kai did not return? Nobody knew where he was, and many tears were shed because people said that he had drowned in the river. Then came spring and at last brought sunshine.

'Kai is dead and gone,' said little Gerda. 'I don't believe it,' answered the sunshine. 'He is dead and gone,' she said to the swallows. 'We don't believe it,' replied the birds, and in the end Gerda did not believe it either.

'I'll put on my new red shoes,' she said one morning, 'and I'll go down to the river and ask about him.' She walked out of the city gates all by herself. 'Is it true that you took my playmate from me? I'll give you my shoes if you bring him back to me!' she said to the river. She took off her shoes and threw them both into the river. But they fell close to the shore, and the waves carried them back on land. Then Gerda climbed into a boat that she saw in the reeds. However, the boat was not moored, and Gerda could not get out in time before it started to drift away. Gerda was frightened and began to cry, but the boat kept drifting down the river. 'Perhaps the boat will carry me to Kai,' thought Gerda, and the thought cheered her up. For many hours, she watched the delightful green banks pass by. Then she came to a large cherry orchard, in which stood a small house. The river carried the boat straight towards the banks, where an old woman came out of the house. She wore a big sun hat that was painted with the loveliest flowers.

'You poor child,' exclaimed the old woman. 'How did you get to be on this rapid river, come and tell me!' she said while pulling the boat out of the water.

Gerda told her everything, and when she asked the woman whether she had seen little Kai, she was told that he had not come by. The woman said that Gerda should not be too sad-dened by this but should instead taste her cher-ries and look at her flowers.

'I have long wished to have a dear little girl like you,' said the old woman. 'You'll see how

> 'Then the Snow Queen kissed little Kai on the forehead. Oh, that kiss felt colder than ice, and its coldness went right to Kai's heart.'

well we'll get on with each other.' Gerda gradually forgot about her playmate, because the old woman knew magic, but she was not a wicked witch.

She led Gerda outside into her flower garden. How glorious the flowers looked, and how fragrant they were! Every flower imaginable stood there in full bloom. Gerda jumped into the air with delight and played until the sun set behind the tall cherry trees.

The next day, she again played among the flowers in the sunshine, and many days went by in this fashion. Gerda knew every flower in the garden, but no matter how many there were, it always seemed to her as if one was missing. One day, she sat looking at the old woman's sun hat, and when she saw the roses on it, tears suddenly streamed from her eyes. She remembered the glorious roses back home, and with them her friend Kai. 'Oh, how long I have been kept,' said the little girl. She went from one flower to the next, asking 'Don't you know where Kai is?' She asked the tiger lilies, trumpet flowers, snowdrops, hyacinths, buttercups, and narcissus flowers, but each only stood in the sun and knew its own story. None knew anything about Kai.

Finally, Gerda ran outside past the garden. She looked back three times, but there was no one following her. When she could no longer run, she sat down on a large rock, and when she looked around, autumn had come. How sore and tired little Gerda's feet were! Everything looked cold and grey around her, and the little girl felt very much alone.

Snow had already fallen here and there, and finally Gerda saw a large crow that had been watching her and cocking its head from side to side. She told the bird everything about her life and asked it whether it had seen little Kai. The crow nodded thoughtfully and said, 'Maybe I have.' 'Do you think?', cried Gerda and almost hugged the crow to death. 'I think I know where he is, but I believe that he would have forgotten you for the princess.' 'Does he live with a princess now?' asked Gerda. 'Yes,' answered the crow. 'I'll tell you as best as I can. In the kingdom where he is lives a princess who is extraordinarily clever. She wished to marry, but only to a man who could give a good answer when one spoke with him; one who does not merely stand around looking lofty. The newspapers published the princess's desire to have all young, handsome men visit the palace to speak with the princess. The one among them who was most handsome and spoke best, as if he was very comfortable with what he was saying, that was the one that she wanted to marry. Yes, yes, believe me, many men flocked to the palace, but not a single one was successful.'

'But Kai!' asked Gerda, 'When did he go there?' 'Wait! On the third day, a small person walked happily towards the palace. His eyes shone like yours, he had long hair, and his clothes were poor.' 'That must have been Kai!' Gerda exclaimed happily.

'He was not intimidated by anything,' said the crow, 'and as he approached, he told the guards that it must be very tiresome to stand on the stairs and that he'd rather go inside.' The crow went on, 'He boldly walked straight up to the princess.' 'And did Kai win the princess?' asked Gerda. 'I want to see for myself, can't you take me to the palace?' 'I'll ask my fiancée, who is a tame crow at the court,' said the bird and flew away.

> 'I think I know where he is, but I believe that he would have forgotten you for the princess.'

The crow only returned late in the evening. 'My love sends you her best wishes. She knows a back staircase that leads to the bedroom of the prince and princess.' Oh, how Gerda's heart beat with fear and longing!

The crow's tame fiancée led them through one of the palace's halls all the way to the bedroom. There were two beds that each looked like a lily. One of them was white, and in it lay the princess. The other was red, and in it Gerda searched for little Kai. She bent one of the red petals to the side, but to her great disappointment she saw that it was not her friend lying in the bed. Little Gerda started to cry and told the prince and princess her story. 'You poor child!' said the prince. Next day, she was dressed in velvet and silk from head to toe, and she was asked whether she wanted to stay at the palace. But Gerda only

asked for a carriage and a horse and a pair of little boots so that she could drive out into the world again to look for Kai.

When she was ready to go, there stood a carriage of pure gold outside the palace gates. 'Farewell!' called the prince, the princess, and the crow. All of them and Gerda cried until the carriage was out of sight.

Gerda drove through a dark forest, but the carriage glowed like a torch and attracted some robbers. They sprang out of the woods, stopped the horses, and pulled little Gerda out of the carriage. 'She is plump and cute,' said an old robber woman, who had a long, bristly beard and eyebrows that hung down over her eyes. 'She is as good as a fat little lamb!' And she pulled out a knife that flashed dreadfully.

'Ouch!' howled the woman at the same moment, because her own daughter, whom she carried on her back, had bitten her ear. 'You ugly brat!' said the mother.

'I want her to play with me,' said the little robber girl. 'I want her to give me her muff and her dress and to sleep in my bed. And I also want to ride in her carriage!' And the little girl was set on having her way. They drove over stumps and stones ever more deeply into the wood. The little robber girl asked, 'You surely must be a princess?'

'No,' said Gerda and told the robber girl everything that had happened to her and how much she loved little Kai. The girl looked at her seriously, nodded a little with her head, and said, 'They shall not kill you – but if I get angry with you I might kill you myself.' Next thing, the carriage stopped, and they had arrived at the courtyard of the robbers' castle.

'You shall sleep with me and my animals tonight,' said the robber girl. They went to a corner strewn with straw and carpets. Above, there were more than a hundred pigeons sitting on sticks and perches.

'They're all mine!' cried the little girl, 'and here is my favorite animal of all, my dear old Bae.'

She pulled a reindeer forward on its horns, and the animal had a copper ring around its neck. 'Every night, I tickle its neck with my knife, and it is very much afraid of that.' And the little girl pulled out a long knife and pushed Gerda towards her bed. 'Will you keep the knife with you while you sleep?' asked Gerda, looking somewhat fearfully at the robber girl. 'Always,' said the little robber girl. 'You never know what might happen.' The girl placed one arm around Gerda's shoulders and kept her knife in the other, and this is how she fell asleep, snoring. But Gerda could not sleep at all.

Then the wood pigeons said to her, 'We have seen little Kai, he was sitting in the Snow Queen's carriage.' 'What is it you are saying up there?' asked Gerda excitedly. 'Where did the Snow Queen travel to?' 'Probably to Lapland, because there is always snow and ice there. Ask the reindeer!' 'That is where the Snow Queen has her summer tent,' said the reindeer, 'but her main palace is on an island called Spitzbergen.'

Next morning, Gerda told the robber girl everything she had heard, and the girl asked the reindeer, 'Do you know where Lapland is?' 'Who would know better than I?' replied the reindeer with sparkling eyes. 'That's where I was born and frolicked about on wide fields of snow.' 'Listen,' said the robber girl, 'Hurry up and take this little girl to the Snow Queen's palace, where her playmate is.'

The reindeer jumped into the air with joy. The little robber girl lifted Gerda up and hoisted her onto the animal's back. 'Here you have your fur boots back,' she said, 'because it'll be very cold, but I'll keep your muff, because it's so very pretty.'

Gerda cried with happiness. 'I don't like it when you cry,' said the little robber girl. 'Now you should be happy instead! And here are two

loaves of bread and a ham.' Gerda reached out to the robber girl and said farewell, and then the reindeer jumped across stumps and stones, through the great forest and over swamps and plains, as fast as it could run. 'There are my beloved northern lights!' said the reindeer. 'See how they glow!' And it ran even faster, day and night, until they reached Lapland.

They stopped outside a small house. There was no one at home apart from an old Lapp woman who was cooking fish in the light of a whale oil lamp, and the reindeer told her Gerda's story.

'You poor things!' cried the Lapp woman. 'You'll have to travel for more than a hundred miles to the Finmark, that's where the Snow Queen lives. I'll write down a few words on a dried codfish; take that with you to the old Finn woman who lives up there. She'll be able to help you better than I can.'

Once Gerda had warmed herself up, the Lapp woman tied her message onto the reindeer and hoisted the girl back up, and off they went again. They saw the most beautiful northern lights throughout the night. When they reached the Finmark, they knocked on the Finn woman's door. She was small and very dirty. The woman immediately read the message that was written on the codfish.

'You are very wise', said the reindeer, 'I know you can tie all of the winds of the world together with a bit of twine. Don't you want to give the little girl a potion that will make her as strong as a dozen men, so that she can overpower the Snow Queen?' The reindeer pleaded so sincerely for little Gerda, and Gerda looked at the old Finn woman with such tearful, imploring eyes that the woman said, 'Little Kai is indeed with the Snow Queen, and he thinks that he is in the best place on earth. But that is because he has a splinter of glass in his heart and a piece of glass in his eye. Unless these are removed, the Snow Queen's power over him will hold.'

'But can't you give Gerda something that gives her power over all of these things?' 'I cannot give her any power that she does not already have. She cannot receive her power from us, because her strength is in her heart. It comes because she is such a dear, innocent child. If she cannot reach the Snow Queen herself and remove the glass from little Kai's heart and eye, there is no help we can give her. The Snow Queen's garden is only two miles from here. That is how far you can carry the girl.' After these words, the reindeer carried Gerda to the garden as fast as its hooves would allow. There were big, hot tears streaming down its face as it left the little girl behind. Poor little Gerda stood there, all by herself in the middle of icy, harsh Finmark.

She ran forward as fast as she could. First she came across an entire regiment of snowflakes, but they did not fall from the sky. Instead, they were alive and ran along the ground, and the closer Gerda came, the larger they grew. These were the Snow Queen's guards. They had the strangest of shapes – knots of snakes twisting their heads or giant, ugly porcupines.

The cold was so intense that little Gerda could see every one of her breaths. Her breath became thicker and thicker and took the shape of little angels, which grew bigger as soon as they touched the ground, and they all wore helmets on their heads and carried shields and lances in their hands. In the end, Gerda was surrounded by an

'Little Kai is indeed with the Snow Queen, and he thinks that he is in the best place on earth.

entire legion of angels. They struck the dreadful snowflakes with their lances, breaking them into a thousand pieces. Little Gerda walked on towards the Snow Queen's palace, fearless and strong.

There, she saw Kai, blue, almost black with cold, but he did not feel a thing. He carried a few icy shards here and there, putting them together any which way he could think of. He arranged them to form all sorts of figures that were to make a written word, but he could never find the right one, which was 'eternity'. The Snow Queen had told him, 'If you can make this word, you shall be your own master.' But he could not do it.

Little Gerda threw her arms around the boy and cried, 'Dearest Kai! I've found you at last!' But Kai sat there all still and stiff. Gerda wept hot tears, which fell onto his chest and went straight to his heart. Her tears thawed the lump of ice his heart had become and washed out the little splinter of glass. Kai looked at Gerda and burst into tears. He cried so much that the splinter of glass in his eye was washed out too, and he finally recognized her and called happily, 'Dearest Gerda! Where have you been for so long?'

He held onto Gerda, who laughed and cried with happiness. Their encounter was so full of joy that even the shards of ice began to dance around them, and when they were tired of dancing, they dropped straight into a pattern making the word 'eternity', and Kai was finally free.

Gerda kissed his cheeks, and the blood returned to them. She kissed his eyes, and the light returned to them. She kissed his hands and feet, and he was well and strong again.

They took each other's hands and wandered out of the palace. They talked about the grandmother and the roses. When they reached the end of the Snow Queen's garden, the reindeer was there waiting for them. It carried the children straight to the border of the northern land, where spring's first green had already appeared. Gerda and Kai kept walking, hand in hand, and wherever they went they were surrounded by beautiful spring, full of flowers and green buds. They heard church bells ring and recognized the tall towers of their hometown. They walked straight to the grandmother's door, up the stairs, and into her room, where everything was still just like they had left it. But when they walked through the door, they realized that they had become adults. They looked into each other's eyes as grown-ups, but in their hearts they were still children. And it was summer, warm glorious summer.

Food to warm your soul

When winter is knocking at our doors and the Snow Queen has decorated our windows with her sparkling crystals, could there be anything better than warming ourselves up in the comfort of our homes with nourishing treats, listening to the magical story of Gerda and Kai?

ENTREE

Crostini with walnuts, blue cheese, and onions

MAIN COURSE

Risotto with roast squash

DESSERT

Crème brûlée with caramelized orange and grapefruit

Celeriac soup
with chorizo

Serves 4

INGREDIENTS

1 orange
400 g (14 oz) celeriac
800 ml (28 fl oz) vegetable stock
100 ml (3½ fl oz) heavy cream
30 g (1 oz) cold butter
1 garlic clove
1 piece fresh ginger
  (about 1 cm/½ inch)
Salt
Freshly ground black pepper

Also:
100 g (3½ oz) chorizo
1 parsley sprig

Wash the orange under hot water, pat dry, and finely grate the zest. Halve and juice the fruit. Peel and dice the celeriac. Bring the vegetable stock to a boil in a saucepan. Reduce the heat to low, add the diced celeriac, and simmer until soft, about 5 minutes. Stir in the cream and butter and blend the soup until smooth with a hand-held blender.

Peel and thinly slice the garlic and ginger. Add them to the soup and simmer everything for a few minutes. Season the soup with the orange zest, salt, and pepper. Blend again briefly before straining the soup through a fine sieve.

Cut the chorizo into thin slices and then into strips. Heat a frying pan and dry-roast the chorizo lightly. Rinse and shake the parsley dry. Pick off the leaves and chop finely. Divide the soup among deep plates or bowls and serve garnished with the chorizo and parsley.

Crostini with walnuts, blue cheese, and onions

Serves 4

INGREDIENTS

2 red onions
1 tbsp sugar
100 ml (3 ½ fl oz) port
  (or red wine)
1 tbsp balsamic vinegar
250 g (9 oz) soft blue cheese
100 g (3 ½ oz) cream cheese
Freshly ground black pepper
50 g (1 ¾ oz) walnuts

Also:

8 small slices of sourdough bread
1 handful of radish or alfalfa
  sprouts (or cress)

Peel and thinly slice the onions. Heat the sugar in a small saucepan and allow it to caramelize slowly. Only stir when the sugar takes on too much color. Keep shaking the pan. Add the onion and deglaze with the port and balsamic vinegar. Simmer for about 5 minutes to reduce. Set the caramelized onion aside to cool.

Preheat the oven to 250°C (500°F). Crumble or dice the blue cheese. Mix the cream cheese until smooth and season with a little pepper. Coarsely chop the walnuts and dry-roast them in a frying pan. Set aside to cool.

Dry-roast the bread slices in a pan until golden brown on both sides. Spread with the seasoned cream cheese and top with a little blue cheese. Transfer the bread to a baking tray. Bake in the preheated oven (middle rack) for 5 minutes to melt the cheese.

Rinse and pat the sprouts dry. Serve the crostini topped with the onion and walnuts, garnished with the sprouts.

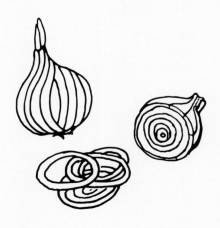

Pasta with radicchio, gorgonzola, and walnuts

Serves 4

INGREDIENTS

3 French shallots
1 tart apple (e.g. Granny Smith)
2 tbsp orange juice
1 small head of radicchio
  (red chicory)
150 g (5½ oz) gorgonzola cheese
2 tbsp olive oil
60 ml (2 fl oz/¼ cup) white wine
100 ml (3½ fl oz) heavy cream
60 g (2¼ oz/¼ cup) cream cheese
Salt
Freshly ground black pepper
300 g (10½ oz) fusilloni
  (large spiral pasta)
40 g (1½ oz) walnuts

Peel and finely dice the shallots. Wash or peel the apple, if preferred. Halve, core, and cut into thin slices and then into julienne strips. Toss the julienned apple with the orange juice.

Wash and trim the radicchio. Pat dry and cut into bite-sized pieces. Finely dice the gorgonzola.

Heat the olive oil in a large pan. Add the shallots and sweat. Add the gorgonzola and deglaze with the white wine. Stir in the cream, cream cheese, and a little salt and pepper and simmer for about 1 minute.

Meanwhile, bring plenty of salted water to a boil in a pot. Cook the fusilloni until al dente according to the instructions on the packet. Add the pasta to the sauce and briefly return everything to a boil. Toss in the radicchio. Coarsely chop the walnuts and dry-roast them in a frying pan.

Divide the pasta and sauce among plates. Garnish with the walnuts and julienned apple and serve.

Lemon chicken with parsley root chips

Serves 4

INGREDIENTS

For the chips:
400 g (14 oz) parsley root
  (Hamburg parsley)
3 tbsp olive oil
½ tsp salt

For the chicken:
1 whole kitchen-ready organic
  chicken (about 1.5 kg/3 lb 5 oz)
2 lemons
2 tbsp olive oil
2 tbsp honey
1 tsp chilli flakes
½ tsp salt
Freshly ground black pepper
3 rosemary sprigs
1 garlic bulb

For the chips, trim and peel the parsley root. Cut the roots into thin strips. This is best done using a mandoline.

Preheat the oven to 180°C (350°F). Line a baking tray with baking paper. Toss the parsley root strips with the olive oil and salt and set aside for 10 minutes, then arrange them on a baking tray in a single layer. Place another sheet of baking paper on top and weigh everything down with another baking tray. Bake the chips in the preheated oven (middle rack) until golden, about 20 minutes. If necessary, turn the baking tray once to ensure that the chips brown evenly.

For the chicken, preheat the oven to 190°C (375°F). Rinse the chicken under cold water and pat it dry. Halve the chicken lengthways. Wash the lemons under hot water, pat dry, and slice them. Whisk the olive oil with the honey, chilli flakes, salt, and a little pepper. Brush the chicken halves with the mixture. Rinse the rosemary and shake it dry. Halve the garlic bulb.

Gently score the chicken skin. Transfer the chicken to a large roasting dish and top it with the lemon slices. Pour 300 ml (10½ fl oz) water into the dish and add the rosemary and garlic. Cook the chicken in the preheated oven (middle rack) until done, about 50 minutes. Serve with the parsley root chips.

Risotto with roast squash

Serves 4

INGREDIENTS

For the roast squash:

1 kabocha squash
1 small red chilli
4 rosemary sprigs
2 garlic cloves
2 tbsp olive oil
1 tbsp honey
Salt
Freshly ground black pepper
1 orange

For the risotto:

3 French shallots
1 tbsp olive oil
240 g (8¾ oz) risotto rice
250 ml (9 fl oz/1 cup) white wine
1 liter (5 cups/34 fl oz) hot
  vegetable stock
2 tbsp butter
2 tbsp finely grated
  parmesan cheese

For the roast squash, preheat the oven to 220°C (425°F). Line a baking tray with baking paper. Wash, trim, and deseed the squash. Cut it into 2 cm (¾ inch) thick wedges. Wash, trim, halve, and deseed the chilli. Chop finely. Rinse the rosemary and shake dry. Pick off and coarsely chop the leaves. Peel and thinly slice the garlic.

Spread the squash wedges on the baking tray, sprinkle them with the chilli, and toss them with the olive oil, rosemary, garlic, and honey. Season with a little salt and pepper. Bake in the preheated oven (bottom rack) until soft, about 30 minutes. Just before the squash is cooked, wash the orange under hot water and pat it dry. Finely peel the zest and cut into very fine matchsticks. Sprinkle the orange zest over the wedges and continue to roast for about another 4 minutes.

Meanwhile, peel and finely chop the shallots for the risotto. Heat the olive oil in a saucepan. Add the shallots and sweat briefly. Stir in the rice and sweat until translucent. Deglaze with the white wine and simmer briefly until the liquid has been absorbed. Add the hot vegetable stock, ladle by ladle, waiting each time until the rice has again absorbed the liquid. Continue to stir frequently. Simmer the risotto until the rice is al dente and creamy.

Dice the butter and stir it into the cooked risotto together with the grated parmesan. Divide the risotto among plates, top with the roasted squash, and serve.

Winter vegetable tart

Serves 6

Makes 1 tart (20 cm/8 inches in diameter)

INGREDIENTS

1 sheet puff pastry
  (about 275 g/9¾ oz)
350 g (12 oz/1½ cups) cream
  cheese
2 large carrots
2 large parsley roots
  (Hamburg parsley)
150 g (5½ oz) Jerusalem
  artichokes
2 red onions
2 garlic cloves
20 g (¾ oz) almonds
2 tbsp olive oil
2 tbsp honey
1 tsp salt
1 orange
1 thyme sprig

Also:
Butter for the dish
Sea salt for sprinkling

Butter a 20 cm (8 inch) flan (tart) dish. Roll out the puff pastry and line the buttered dish with the pastry. Fold in any overhanging edges. Whisk the cream cheese until smooth and spread it evenly across the tart base.

Trim and peel the carrots, parsley roots, and Jerusalem artichokes. Slice the vegetables thinly; this is best done with a mandoline. Peel and thinly slice the onions and garlic. Coarsely chop the almonds. Transfer all of the prepared ingredients to a mixing bowl and toss them with the olive oil, honey, and salt. Halve and juice the orange. Rinse and pat dry the thyme, then pick off the leaves. Toss the vegetables with the orange juice and thyme. Set aside to marinate for 10 minutes.

Meanwhile, preheat the oven to 190°C (375°F). Spread the vegetables evenly on top of the cream cheese. Bake the tart in the preheated oven (middle rack) until the vegetables are cooked but still have a little bite, about 50 minutes. Serve sprinkled with sea salt.

Black bean, chilli, and meatball stew

Serves 4

INGREDIENTS

For the stew:

250 g (9 oz) dried black beans
1 red onion
1 red chilli
1 tbsp butter
1 tbsp mustard
1 tbsp tomato paste
½ tsp Worcestershire sauce
300 ml (10½ fl oz) tomato
  sauce (ketchup)
Salt

For the meatballs:

1 bread roll
2 French shallots
2 tbsp olive oil, divided
2 parsley sprigs
1 mint sprig
400 g (14 oz) minced (ground)
  lamb (or beef)
1 egg
1 egg yolk
1 pinch salt
Freshly ground black pepper

Also:

2 parsley sprigs
Chilli flakes for garnish

For the stew, soak the beans in cold water overnight. The next day, drain the beans in a strainer and rinse them under cold water. Peel and finely dice the onion. Wash, trim, halve, and deseed the chilli. Chop finely.

Heat the butter in a saucepan. Add the onion and sweat briefly. Stir in the mustard, tomato paste, and Worcestershire sauce, followed by the tomato sauce and 300 ml (10½ fl oz) water. Add the beans and cover but leave the lid slightly ajar. Cook until the beans are soft, about 70 minutes. Season the stew with salt and chilli.

For the meatballs, soak the bread roll in water for 5 minutes. Squeeze out any excess water and chop finely. Peel and finely dice the shallots. Heat 1 tbsp olive oil in a frying pan. Add the shallots and sweat. Rinse the parsley and mint, shake dry, and finely chop the leaves. Add the herbs to the shallots, then remove the pan from the heat.

Place the lamb, egg, egg yolk, soaked bread roll, and shallot and herb mixture into a mixing bowl. Combine well and season with salt and pepper. Shape the meat mixture into small balls. Heat the remaining oil in a large ovenproof frying pan. Fry the meatballs until completely browned. If necessary, continue to cook for about another 5 minutes in an oven preheated to 180°C (350°F).

Rinse and shake the parsley dry. Pick off the leaves and chop. Divide the stew and meatballs among deep plates or bowls and garnish with parsley and chilli flakes to serve.

Minestrone

Serves 4

INGREDIENTS

1 onion
2 garlic cloves
100 g (3½ oz) green
   cabbage leaves
½ celeriac
2 carrots
6 slices bacon
2 tbsp olive oil
100 ml (3½ fl oz) white wine
Salt
Freshly ground black pepper
1 bay leaf
2 thyme sprigs
1.5 liters (52 fl oz/6 cups)
   vegetable stock
400 g (14 oz) canned
   peeled tomatoes

Also:
40 g (1½ oz) parmesan
   cheese, grated

Peel and thinly slice the onion and garlic. Wash and pat dry the cabbage leaves. Remove the core and slice thinly. Peel the celeriac and carrots and cut into 1 cm (½ inch) cubes. Finely dice the bacon.

Heat the olive oil in a saucepan. Add the onion, garlic, and bacon and sweat briefly. Stir in the prepared celeriac, carrot, and cabbage. Fry briefly, then deglaze with the white wine. Season the vegetables with salt and pepper. Stir in the bay leaf, thyme, vegetable stock, and tomatoes and bring everything to a boil. Simmer the soup for about 20 minutes.

Remove the bay leaf, then divide the minestrone soup among deep plates or bowls and serve sprinkled with parmesan.

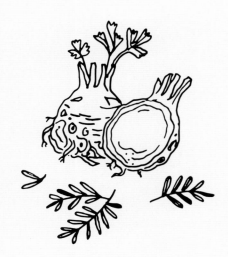

Crème brûlée
with caramelized orange
and grapefruit

**Makes 4 ramekins
(200 ml/7 fl oz each)**

INGREDIENTS

For the crème brûlée:
*50 g (1¾ oz) sugar
250 ml (9 fl oz/1 cup)
  heavy cream
300 ml (10½ fl oz) milk
1 vanilla bean
6 egg yolks*

**For the caramelized orange
and grapefruit:**
*1 orange
1 pink grapefruit
50 g (1¾ oz) sugar*

Also:
*50 g (1¾ oz) caster
  (superfine) sugar*

For the crème brûlée, heat the sugar in a large frying pan or wide saucepan (about 30 cm/12 inches in diameter) and allow it to caramelize slowly. Only stir when the sugar takes on too much color. Keep shaking the pan.

Warm the cream and milk until lukewarm. Slice the vanilla bean open lengthways and scrape out the seeds. Stir the cream and milk mixture and the vanilla bean and seeds into the caramelized sugar in the pan. Simmer everything for about 2 minutes over a low heat, then set aside for 10 minutes to cool until lukewarm.

Preheat the oven to 90°C (195°F). Whisk the egg yolks and stir the lukewarm cream mixture into the yolks. Keep whisking to combine everything well, then pass the mixture through a fine sieve. Divide the cream among the ramekins and cook them in the preheated oven (middle rack) for about 1½ hours. Set aside to cool, then refrigerate, preferably overnight.

For the caramelized orange and grapefruit, peel and slice the fruit. Caramelize the sugar using the method described above. Add the orange and grapefruit slices. Coat them in the caramel and remove the pan from the heat. Leave the citrus slices to marinate and cool for 10 minutes.

Sprinkle the crème brûlée with sugar and use a blow torch to caramelize. Alternatively, caramelize in a preheated oven (250°C/500°F, top heat). Serve with the caramelized orange and grapefruit.

Berry pavlova
with vanilla cream

Serves 4

INGREDIENTS

For the pavlova:
4 egg whites, chilled
210 g (7½ oz) caster
  (superfine) sugar
1 dash lemon juice
1 pinch cornflour (cornstarch)

For the vanilla cream:
1 vanilla bean
250 ml (9 fl oz/1 cup)
  heavy cream
20 g (¾ oz) icing
  (confectioners') sugar

Also:
250 g (9 oz) mixed berries
  (e.g. raspberries, redcurrants,
  blackberries, and blueberries)
Icing (confectioners') sugar
  for dusting

For the pavlova, use an electric mixer with the whisk attachment to beat the egg whites until they form soft peaks. As the egg whites firm up, gradually pour in the sugar, whisking continuously. Gently fold in the lemon juice and cornflour.

Preheat the oven to 110°C (225°F). Line a baking tray with baking paper. Spread the egg white mixture in an even circle (about 20 cm/8 inches in diameter) on the baking paper. Bake the pavlova in the preheated oven (middle rack) until it is dry to the touch, about 70–80 minutes. Turn off the oven and leave the pavlova in the oven with the door ajar to cool completely.

For the vanilla cream, slice the vanilla bean open lengthways and scrape out the seeds. Whip the cream until stiff. Whisk in the vanilla seeds and icing sugar.

Pick through the berries. Rinse gently, if necessary, and pat dry. Spread the vanilla cream over the cooled pavlova base and top with the berries. Serve the pavlova dusted with icing sugar.

White Irish Cream mousse

**Makes 4 bowls
(about 100 ml/3½ fl oz each)**

<u>INGREDIENTS</u>

2 leaves gelatine
120 g (4¼ oz) white chocolate
1 egg
50 ml (1½ fl oz) Baileys Irish
  Cream
250 ml (9 fl oz/1 cup)
  heavy cream

Also:
2 tbsp pistachio kernels
½ pineapple
3 tbsp sugar

Soak the gelatine in cold water for 5 minutes. Finely chop the chocolate and melt it in a double boiler over a low heat. Crack the egg into a metal bowl and beat it until thick and creamy in another double boiler over a low heat.

Warm the Baileys Irish Cream in a small saucepan over a low heat. Remove the gelatine from the water and squeeze out the liquid. Whisk the gelatine into the warm Baileys to dissolve, making sure that the liqueur is not too hot! Stir the Baileys and gelatine mixture into the egg yolk together with the warm, melted chocolate. Leave everything to cool to about 35°C (95°F).

Meanwhile, whip the cream until stiff, then fold it into the chocolate and Baileys mixture. Divide the cream among bowls or jars and refrigerate for at least 6 hours or overnight.

Coarsely chop the pistachios. Remove the pineapple skin. Quarter the pineapple, remove the core, and cut it into wedges. Heat the sugar in a small saucepan and allow it to caramelize slowly. Only stir when the sugar takes on too much color. Keep shaking the pan. Add the pineapple pieces and pistachios to the pan and toss them in the caramel for a few minutes until the pineapple is slightly browned.

Serve the white chocolate mousse with the caramelized pineapple and pistachios.

Index

The Team

Recipe development and food styling

Alexander Höss-Knakal was born in Vienna and lives in Klosterneuburg, Austria. He learned his trade with renowned Michelin-starred restaurants and has worked as a freelance food stylist and recipe developer since 1997. His recipes impress with carefully chosen ingredients and exquisite combinations, and they are a pure delight for both the palate and the eyes. He shares his extensive knowledge not only through his cookbooks and magazine contributions, but also in cooking classes.

hoessknakal.com

Text

Julia Bauer has worked as an editor, project manager, and ghost-writer for fifteen years. She learned her trade with a publishing house that specializes in cooking and cuisine. She became an expert for cookbooks through her close collaboration with star chefs, pâtissiers, and master pastry chefs, and throughout her career her passion for good texts, good books, and good food has only grown.

julia-bauer.berlin

Photography

Melina Kutelas started her career as a fashion stylist in London but was then drawn back to her hometown of Vienna in 2014. In 2015, she launched her own food blog and started to work as a food photographer and stylist soon after.

aboutthatfood.com

Layout

Andrea Högerle studied graphic design in Pforzheim, Germany. Her fascination for the UK led her to finish her studies at Leeds University. Following various stints in the Netherlands, she and her partner, Simon Jefferson, established a visual communications agency in Cologne together.

jefferson-hoegerle.com

Visit our website at www.skyhorsepublishing.com.

10 9 8 7 6 5 4 3 2 1

Library of Congress Cataloging-in-Publication Data is available on file.

Cover design by Madeleine Kane

Print ISBN: 978-1-5107-7003-4
Ebook ISBN: 978-1-5107-7004-1

Printed in China

OVEN GUIDE: You may find cooking times vary depending on the oven you are using. For fan-forced ovens,
as a general rule, set the oven temperature to 20°C (70°F) lower than indicated in the recipe.

TABLESPOON MEASURES: We have used 20 ml (4 teaspoon) tablespoon measures. If you are using a 15 ml
(3 teaspoon) tablespoon add an extra teaspoon of the ingredient for each tablespoon specified.